Rachel's Tears

The Spiritual Journey
of Columbine Martyr
Rachel Scott

7891740691

DARRELL SCOTT AND BETH NIMMO
with Steve Rabey

THOMAS NELSON PUBLISHERS®
Nashville

Published in Nashville, Tennessee, by Thomas Nelson, Inc.

ISBN 0-7852-6848-0

Printed in the United States of America
03 04 05 PHX 22 21

We would like to dedicate this book to the loving memory of the thirteen beloved people who were the victims of the most deadly school shooting in American history. God gave them all life, but this gift was extinguished far too early.

Dave Sanders

Like many of the teachers and staff at Columbine, Dave risked his life to protect his students. When he heard the sound of gunshots in the school, Dave didn't run for his life, but shouted out an alarm so others could protect themselves. Then he bravely herded all the students he could find to safety. His actions may have saved hundreds of lives that day, but his selfless sacrifice cost him his own life.

Serving at Columbine for twenty-five years, Dave was a beloved business teacher and the coach of the girls' basketball team. He inspired his students to do their best through both his life and his death. As he lay dying from his gunshot wounds, Dave asked students to hold pictures of his wife and his two daughters before his eyes. He was focusing on those images as he passed from the chaos of that day into eternity.

Cassie Bernall

Cassie's mother wrote a book describing this young woman's struggles with destructive beliefs and negative self-esteem as well as the dramatic change she underwent that shaped the final years of her life. Her unquenchable faith in God exposed her to ridicule at school and may have contributed to her death, but her unshakable dedication has helped her become an internationally recognized symbol of Christian commitment.

Steven Curnow

A freshman student who excelled at soccer, Steven loved aviation. His dream was to join the navy and become a pilot of an F-16. He was also an avid *Star Wars* fan. The new *Star Wars* movie was scheduled to debut on May 19, 1999, and Steven was eagerly anticipating seeing it. He was a friendly young man who was known for his big smile.

Corey DePooter

An amiable boy who loved America and hoped to serve his country as a marine, Corey spent part of Tuesday morning showing friends pamphlets that a military recruiter had given him. Mature beyond his years and cool and collected under pressure, Corey sought to calm nervous students who huddled with him as the killers roamed the school. Friends brought fishing tackle and gear to his funeral in memory of his love of the outdoors.

Kelly Fleming

Quiet and somewhat shy, Kelly expressed herself well on paper. She was writing the story of her life when she was killed. Her dad lovingly remarked that when they killed his daughter, they killed innocence. She was just learning to drive and wanted to get a job at a day care center so she could save up money for a Mustang or a Corvette. She had a passion for writing and wanted to pursue that as a career.

Matthew Kechter

The night before he was killed, Matt was up until midnight talking on the phone to our son Craig, who was one of his closest friends. A friendly boy with an infectious sense of humor, Matt had hoped to land a starting spot on Columbine's football team. The following fall, when the team won its first state title, the victory was dedicated to Matt. As committed to academics as he was to athletics, Matt died next to Craig in the library that day.

Daniel Mauser

Danny had just been named the top biology student at Columbine for the school year, but he never knew that he won the honor because he was killed in the library days before it was announced. A smart, quiet boy who excelled at forensics as well as math and science, he had received straight A's on his last report card. He had been planning to visit France in the summer after school was out.

Daniel Rohrbough

A hardworking boy who helped out at a family business during the school year and at his grandfather's Kansas farm in the summer, Danny used the money he made to buy gifts and presents for others and was universally hailed as unselfish and caring. A good athlete and dedicated weight lifter, Danny was killed outside Columbine. When he didn't show up for work that afternoon, his parents grew worried, only to see his life-less body on the cover of the next morning's newspapers.

Isaiah Shoels

Isaiah was a friend of our son Craig. He had played corner-back on the school's football team, where he was known for his tenacity. Small in stature but large in heart and spirit, he held his own with larger players. He was killed next to our son under a table in the library. Some of Craig's worst memories of April 20, 1999, are of hearing racial slurs flung at Isaiah for several minutes before he was murdered. Isaiah dreamed of becoming a music executive.

John Tomlin

John and Doreen Tomlin have become some of my (Darrell) closest friends. Their son, John, was killed in the library. His Chevy truck became one of the two vehicles seen worldwide as monuments of the tragedy. Rachel's red Acura Legend was the other. John's open Bible on the dashboard of his truck was a testimony of his beliefs to all who saw it. He had spent time in Mexico helping build housing for the poor and doing mission work. Weeks before his death, John's mother had asked him where he would want to be buried if anything ever happened to him. Because of that conversation, he is buried in Wisconsin where his two close childhood friends live.

Lauren Townsend

Potential valedictorian of her senior class, Lauren was a member of the National Honor Society and served as captain of the Columbine girls' varsity volleyball team. A gifted student who had recently visited England with other members of an advanced English class, Lauren worked at an animal shelter, and she planned to study wildlife biology at college in the fall.

Kyle Velasquez

A dedicated Denver Broncos fan, Kyle was often called a "gentle giant." Kyle manifested a simple sincerity and a kind heart. He was buried with military honors at Fort Logan National Cemetery. His dad was a U.S. Navy veteran. Kyle was working on a computer in the library when he was cruelly gunned down.

Rachel Joy Scott

Our beautiful daughter's unique life and deep commitment to God are explored in the following pages.

The two perpetrators of these horrible killings took their own lives that tragic day. We ask that you pray for the Klebold and Harris families, who have been subjected to their own unimaginable grief.

Contents

Foreword
Josh McDowell

I watched in horror as the tragedy in Littleton, Colorado, unfolded on April 20, 1999. As a parent, I could not even begin to comprehend the terrible pain that was to become the daily companion of the family members of the young people killed or injured that day.

I have been moved to get to know Darrell Scott and Beth Nimmo, parents of Rachel Joy Scott, in the midst of their terrible journey. They both deeply loved their daughter. They struggled to be good parents. They watched their daughter as she grew in her faith through moments of deep questioning and steps of profound insight and wisdom. They thought they had a future full of watching her fulfill her dreams. And then in a moment she was lost to them here on earth forever.

Now, through *Rachel's Tears,* they share how God has given them the grace to allow Him to transform this tragedy into triumph. I am grateful that Darrell and Beth are boldly using their story to heal young people and parents and to give new hope for the future to our nation.

Foreword

Wes Yoder

Are you watching the breaking news from Columbine High School?" was the first thing I heard when I called a friend who is a news producer at CNN headquarters in Atlanta on that day we will never forget as long as we live. No horror quite like this had visited us before. We hoped and prayed it would never visit us again.

Every generation seems to lose its innocence, in one way or another, at the wrong time. For this generation, no loss had ever been more personal or come with such devastating finality. Those under the age of thirty had never seen a day more dark. We shivered as the chill enveloped us.

As a nation, we watched the moment-by-moment replay of a tragedy, as the face of evil was unmasked before us. We gasped in horror. What we saw was a reflection of our own marred image. In that tragic hour, the soul of our nation was pierced, and the raw terror of our own barbarism made us shudder and weep.

Now, a year later, perhaps what we should fear most is that our pain should pass on into the night too quickly. Borne on the wings of pain and suffering come many of life's greatest treasures, and these treasures become for us the non-negotiables of our existence on the worn soil of this old world. Forget the lessons and squander the treasures, and they must be learned again and again. Keep them, and they will be ours forever.

I have had the honor of meeting many of the parents and some of the students and friends of those whose lives were destroyed at Columbine. In each one there is a quiet and sacred place, a holy determination that their children, their brothers and sisters, and their friends must not have died in vain. This, for them, is about much more than learning to suffer with dignity and grace.

And that, in part, is the reason for this book. Darrell and Beth, as broken as they have been, as many tears as they still pour over their daughter's grave and onto the shoulders of their children and friends, have found a place of strength and hope. From their broken hearts, the sounds of a new song are being heard. It is a song about love and forgiveness and kindness they pray will be carried as healing to others experiencing sorrow and loss in whatever form they come. Perhaps what they have learned will prevent similar grief for others. "Kindness," as Darrell says, "is the best antidote for violence."

It is my most sincere prayer that we, the people of this great and mighty nation, will not lose the qualities that have made us great—the respect, honor, and dignity afforded to everyone from the least to the greatest where the weak and the strong seek the good of each other as brothers and sisters. And to you, dear Columbine, may God's grace comfort and sustain you always!

Introduction
The Book We Didn't Want to Write

RACHEL JOY SCOTT

We are thankful that you are reading this book, but we hope you understand that it is a book we never wanted to write.

The horrible tragedy at Columbine has turned things absolutely upside down for us and for the other families and loved ones of the thirteen people who were killed and the many more who were injured that day in April 1999.

Since then, this unimaginable event has struck a nerve with people around the world as many have struggled to come to grips with America's worst school shooting. A writer for the magazine *Christianity Today* said, "This event is becoming a defining moment for this generation of teens."

In the past year, we have been repeatedly interviewed by

the national media, we have met world leaders and renowned entertainers, and we have spoken to thousands upon thousands of people at schools, churches, and town hall meetings.

We do all this because we believe that our daughter Rachel Scott has a powerful message that survives her tragic death and needs to be heard by everyone.

Sorrow and Serenity

In everything we do, our deep sense of calling is mingled with a profound sense of sadness. The speeches we have given and the words that appear on these pages have been mixed with innumerable tears.

We wish we didn't have to do any of this. This whole episode has been a cause of great pain and great loss in our lives. We would drop everything in an instant if we could have Rachel with us once again, or if we could have kept our son Craig from experiencing the horrors he endured that day in the Columbine library.

At the same time, even though we never would have chosen to live through the last year, we *have* lived through it, and we now have a powerful conviction that God had a purpose in the way that Rachel's life unfolded.

As you will see, Rachel had a growing sense that she did not have long to live. We picked up only inklings of this while she was alive, but it all became crystal clear to us in the weeks and months after her death as we read the many journals she had written.

Letters to God

Some people cry out to God in prayer. Others reach out to God through singing, playing music, or creating works of art. Rachel did all of these things, but more than anything, she poured out her heart to God through writing in her journals.

In 1997, Beth gave Rachel a small journal for Christmas. That very day, Rachel wrote a prayer to God on page one. Reading that prayer today, you can see the simple and joyous intimacy she had with God, telling Him about her plans for the journal, and thanking Him for the birth of His Son nearly two thousand years ago. Over the next sixteen months, Rachel would write hundreds of letters to God, leaving us with a record of her love for her Lord.

After her death, we found her many journals, which overflow with her prayers, her doubts, her ever-evolving sense of purpose and calling, and her growing sense that her days on this earth were numbered.

You will be reading portions of her private journals and seeing some of the drawings she made on their pages. Our purpose isn't to hold Rachel up as some kind of perfect, sinless saint because she was as frail and fallen as all of us, as her brothers and sisters are well aware.

Rather, we share these things because we believe her brief life holds powerful lessons for all of us, including young people, for whom she cared so much, and parents, many of whom struggle with how to instill deep and lasting godly values in their children.

During the last year, we have learned a few other lessons from Rachel's brief life and sudden death, lessons we will be sharing with you.

> December 25, 97
>
> Dear God,
>   Thank you!!! Thank you
> for my mom, my mom who gave
> me this journal so that I may
> write you. Thank you for my
> family, my friends, and my youth.
> my words will be said to
> you thru my writings. I write
> to you now thanking you.
> Today we recognize the
> birth of your Son, Jesus. I
> thank you for Him. He was
> born to us, so that He may
> die for us. Thank you. I love
> you Father. I love you because
> of your grace, your righteosness,
> your forgiveness, your love.
>   Amen

Living the Life

Rachel loved God, and she had an overpowering urge to communicate that love to everyone she knew. She didn't beat people over the head with her Bible, and she never coerced anyone into faith. Instead, she shared her faith by living her life to the full, praying that others would see the divine light that burned so brightly within her heart.

We hope that by telling Rachel's story, we can help those who knew her to have a greater understanding of her inner spiritual motivations. We also hope those who didn't know her can be inspired by her example.

Resting in God's Hands

Through the events of the past year, we have come to a deeper understanding of something theologians call the sovereignty of God.

Everyone wrestles with questions about good and evil, asking how God can permit bad things to happen in the world. We continue to wrestle with these same issues, and we certainly don't have all the answers. But in some ways, the losses we have endured have helped us experience a deeper level of trust in God and a more accepting faith that He knows exactly what He is doing.

This is a painful thing to say, of course, for no parent wants to go through the soul-wrenching things that we and the other Columbine parents have endured.

At the same time, we know that Rachel prayed that she would make an impact on the world. She wanted to serve God with all her heart. And her willingness to die for her faith has already had a powerful impact on thousands and thousands of young people around the world who have heard us talk about her message.

The ways of God are mysterious, but we believe that God sovereignly prepared Rachel for her own death, providing her with an increasingly clear awareness that the end was near. In fact, during the final hours before she and others were shot, Rachel drew a prophetic picture in her journal showing her eyes crying thirteen tears that were watering a rose. She also had a brief talk with a girlfriend named

Lindsay, during which Rachel said she felt something very strange about the day.

Rachel may have been concerned and possibly even fearful. But as she did in other cases, she clung to God, believing that He was with her in the present moment and would be with her until the very end. We believe her faith in God and her submission to His will provide an inspiring model that more of us should emulate.

Forgiving the Unforgivable

People respond differently to tragedy when it strikes their lives. Some never get over it. Others become bitter and angry, and that is easily understandable. However, we are given the opportunity to experience a realm of grace that is incomprehensible to some when we choose to forgive. Were we angry when our daughter was killed? Yes! Were we sad? Beyond description! But are we forgiving? That is probably one of the most difficult issues to face when you have been so deeply wronged.

Our understanding of God's heart left us only one choice, the decision to forgive. It was the choice of Jesus as He hung on a cross dying. He said in Matthew 5:43–44: "You have heard that it was said, 'Love your neighbor and hate your enemy.' But I tell you: Love your enemies and pray for those who persecute you."

Forgiveness is not just for the offender. It is also for the one who is offended. If we do not forgive, we end up in perpetual anger and bitterness and eventually offend others with our words or actions. If we forgive, we experience a "letting go" or cleansing process that frees us from the offender.

There is a great misunderstanding about forgiveness. Forgiveness is not pardon. Forgiveness is an attitude, while pardon is an action. Had they lived, we would not have pardoned these boys for what they did. In fact, I (Darrell) would have killed them to prevent the slaughter that occurred if I had been given the chance. I believe most people would have done the same. If they had lived, we would have testified against them and demanded that justice be done. However, our hearts toward them could not have harbored unforgiveness. Unforgiveness blocks God's ability to flow through us to help others.

It was this attitude of forgiveness that caught the attention of people such as Maria Shriver, Tom Brokaw, and Larry King. It produced positive remarks from people such as Rosie O'Donnell, who stated that she was brought to her knees in the face of such grace. We say this, not to gloat, but to illustrate that forgiveness brings positive response from others. We also recognize that many of the other victims' families from the Columbine tragedy expressed a heart of forgiveness as well.

God wants us to overcome evil with good. Such a thing is beyond human ability, but it is possible when we acknowledge our weakness and submit to God's grace. It is our prayer that this book will help sow the seeds of grace and forgiveness in your heart as you read the incredible story of our precious daughter Rachel.

An Improbable "Saint"

If Rachel were alive today, she would get a big laugh out of the fact that people were reading her journals and looking at her as if she were a Christian role model.

Still, we believe she would be pleased that you're reading these pages right now. A passion for God, a compassion for others, and a deep desire to be an instrument of God's grace were cornerstones of her life. She would be gratified to see seeds of commitment and forgiveness being planted in the heart of everyone who reads this book.

Sincerely,

Darrell Scott and Beth Nimmo

Rachel's Tears

1 "Halls of Tragedy"

COLUMBINE HIGH SCHOOL

The events of April 20, 1999, have generated miles of print in newspapers and magazines and months' worth of coverage on TV and radio all over the world.

The televised images of frightened children running from a school surrounded by dozens of police clothed in bullet-proof vests and armed with high-caliber weapons were instantly broadcast around the globe and remain a chilling testimony of the terrible events that unfolded that day.

Nearly everyone now knows that two troubled teens who were overcome with hatred and a desire for revenge lashed out at their peers at Columbine High School, a school of nearly nineteen hundred students located eight miles southwest of Denver, Colorado. When the smoke cleared, twelve young people and one teacher were dead, nearly two dozen

1

more were injured, and hundreds more were traumatized by the hellish sights and sounds they experienced.

Investigators had to use extreme caution in analyzing the crime, and what they found was at least as shocking as the shootings themselves. The two boys had planted nearly one hundred explosive devices in and around the school. Most of the bombs never went off, but if they had, they could have taken hundreds more innocent lives.

In the year since that fateful day, Columbine has become a potent symbol of the alienation and violence that can often lie hidden beneath the seemingly tranquil surface of contemporary American life. The tragedy has been endlessly dissected by various experts, civic leaders, and religious figures seeking to find some sense of resolution among all the pain and chaos.

What is less well known is how that fateful day was experienced by those who were closest to the tragedy. In the following pages, Darrell and Beth recount the emotional roller coaster they rode as the day's events unfolded.

Then they tell how their discovery of Rachel's journals led to new insights into their daughter's intense spiritual life. As they reviewed the writings and drawings that Rachel had kept private to herself and God, they came to a deeper understanding of her all-encompassing faith as well as her premonitions of her death.

In a journal entry, Rachel eerily described the corridors of Columbine as "halls of tragedy." As painful as it is for Rachel's parents to relive the memories of what happened on April 20, 1999, they form a necessary prelude to the story of a young girl's amazing spiritual pilgrimage that will be told in the rest of this book.

Beth

Then two will be in the field; one will be taken and one will be left.
—Matthew 24:40 NRSV

The dawn broke over our hometown of Littleton that fateful morning of Tuesday, April 20, 1999, just as it had so many times before. What began as an ordinary school day at our household in a typical middle-class neighborhood just blocks away from Columbine High School gave me no hint of the storm clouds gathering over my home, my family, my city, and ultimately my world. I could never have imagined, as I went through the usual motions of getting my children up and ready for school that morning, that before this day was over, my heart would be shredded and my familiar world left shattered. On this day, my precious seventeen-year-old daughter, Rachel Joy Scott, would be cruelly martyred for her faith in Jesus Christ and go to heaven.

I ran downstairs and knocked on the bedroom doors of Rachel and her younger brother Craig, telling them that they needed to get up right away. I put in a load of laundry and ran back upstairs to tap on my youngest son Mike's door to remind him of the time. The routine was familiar, and I'd give almost anything to be able to go back and live out that familiar pace again, but I know I can never go back. I got myself ready for work, and a few minutes later, ran down the stairs again to check on the kids, making sure they were moving around. After a second knock and call to Rachel, I returned upstairs.

Rachel had a heavy schedule on Mondays, working at the Subway sandwich shop after school, and then after work going to her youth cell group, which lasted late into the evening. On most Tuesday mornings it was hard for her to get up for that 7:20 A.M. class. There was always so much activity in Rachel's life at that time, and an evening at home for her was becoming rare. In the previous month she had been at her school play rehearsal almost every school night. My mother's heart was concerned that Rachel was getting too tired.

It was only a matter of minutes before I heard Rachel tapping on my bathroom door: "Mom, may I come in?" I knew what would come next. Rachel would drag out my makeup bag and start pulling out her favorite cosmetics. As with many teenagers, Rachel's own personal makeup could be any number of places—her backpack, car, or purse or with a friend—but she could always count on Mom's makeup to be in the same place every time. Even though I would sometimes pretend to be exasperated, I actually enjoyed having this little bit of "girl time" with her every morning. How I yearn to hear that tapping on my bathroom door and her sweet voice again.

There was a game that the kids and I would play at times. It was one where they would be the parent and I would be the selfish, rebellious, bratty kid. I loved this game because I could show them just how they acted at times. I always got into this role and loved giving them a hard time. As usual, Rachel and I started bantering in our play-acting, and before I knew it, her brothers Craig and Michael joined in. It was amazing how the wit and satire would start to flow.

I don't recall the actual conversation that morning, but I remember as if it were seared into my mind one of the last things Rachel said to me before she left the bathroom: "Mom, I just don't know what I am going to do with you. I am not going to be able to take care of you anymore." Another impression that I hold dear in my memory of that last morning we had together was how beautiful Rachel looked. I remember in detail what clothes she had on, and I thought, *You know, she is so unaware of how pretty she is.* How could I have known that my memory of her clothes would become so important later that day?

In the next minute or two, Rachel was calling out to Craig to hurry up or they were going to be late for class. It's a cross we bear in our family that Craig is usually late, and we regularly end up waiting for him. It was the source of more than one argument on school mornings. Within minutes, they were out the door and into Rachel's little red Acura, which she had sweetly convinced her stepfather, Larry, that she just had to have.

After dropping Mike off at his school, I went to work. The day was busy, and before I knew where the time had gone, it was after 11:00 A.M. The office phone rang, and I picked it up. Much to my surprise it was my oldest daughter, Bethanee. I could hear panic and fear in her voice. She said, "Mom, something terrible is happening at Columbine. I'm going to go down there and get Craig and Rachel."

She frantically told me to turn on the news, and I immediately turned off my CD and tuned in a news station. My heart began to race as I heard the newscaster describe a vicious attack occurring at Columbine High School! *Rachel! Craig!* My thoughts raced as I tried to make sense of what I was hearing. I called my husband, Larry, on his cell phone and told him to turn on the news. I then ran into my boss's office and said, "I may need to leave work." I blurted, "Something is happening at Columbine, and on the radio they are requesting that parents come and get their students." Of course, my boss said, "Beth, do what you need to do." I called Larry back and asked him to come and pick me up right away. We needed to get to our children!

While I waited anxiously for Larry, I had another call. A momentary rush of relief came over me. It was my sixteen-year-old son, Craig. The conversation didn't last long, but his words were chilling. He said, "Mom, I'm okay and safe, but this is bad, Mom, really, really bad. I have been praying with kids outside the school that may have brothers or sisters still in there that they will get out safe, but, Mom, I can't find Rachel. Mom, I have a real bad feeling about Rachel, and, Mom, we have to pray for her. This is bad, Mom, and we need to pray for Rachel!" He repeated that more than once, and then he said he had to get off the phone because he had borrowed a cell phone to call me and other kids were waiting to use it.

Seconds after I said good-bye to Craig and hung up, Larry ran into my office. Parents were being directed to two pickup points where students were being bused in. One was Leawood Elementary School, and the other was the Columbine Public Library. Larry had been in conversation by cell phone with Rachel's father, Darrell, and since he was going to Leawood, we decided to go to the library. We had to park some distance away because everything was blocked off and emergency and police vehicles were everywhere. Half walking and half running, we arrived at the library and were immediately overwhelmed by what seemed to be total confusion.

Parents and kids alike were huddled around crying, hugging, and telling what had happened. There was an officer or someone from emergency services standing on a chair asking people to listen as he tried to give out information. Lists of students who were safe and accounted for were being announced, and of course, many parents were calling out the names of their children to find out if they were listed. As I look back, this whole experience seems so unreal. Already stores and fast-food services had started bringing in food, drinks, and water. Representatives from all over the community were there to offer counseling and support to students and parents. There was a TV broadcasting on-site news. However, parents were being encouraged not to watch the TV because the situation was somewhat out of control and nothing was being confirmed.

The afternoon dragged on and on. Rachel had just finished performing in the high school play about ten days before, and I recognized some of the other student performers in the library. I went up to one young man named Sergio and told him who I was and asked if he had seen Rachel or knew of anyone who had information about her. His eyes filled with tears, and he said no one had seen her. He said if he got any news, he would be sure to let me know. I went back and sat down in a chair where I had spent much of the afternoon. On and off through the day, I overheard unbelievable accounts of the students' various experiences.

The later it got into the afternoon, the more my concern grew. Around 5:00 P.M., the crowd in the library was thinning. Buses had been bringing in students and as they were being united with their parents, people were leaving. After a while the authorities announced that all remaining parents should go to Leawood, as there would be no more buses coming to the library.

Larry and I hurried back to our car and started on the detour set up by the police to get to the school. Darrell, Rachel's dad, and Larry had been keeping up with each other by cell phone during the day. Jefferson County school authorities had called for a mandatory lockdown of all the schools in the area because of the Columbine emergency, so my youngest son, Mike, had to be signed out by my eldest daughter,

Bethanee, before he could be released from Ken Caryl Middle School. Bethanee and her husband, Don, had gone to our house. Rachel's sister Dana had come from her work, and Craig was finally at home. We felt we had all our bases covered if anyone received a call from Rachel.

We found parking as close to Leawood as possible, and we were amazed at the news media that had set up camp with their trucks, satellite dishes, and cameras. We walked past the governor giving an interview, and approached the entrance of the school. The first people I recognized were my brother-in-law, Larry Scott, and a co-church worker, Ray Feidt. Larry had two children, Jeff and Sarah, at Columbine. They had made it out safely. He put his arm around me and said, "Beth, this does not look good."

We were taken into a room and asked to sit down. People were everywhere, but I had not seen Darrell yet. Coming into the room a few minutes later, Isaiah Shoels's parents sat with us. We were in this room about ten minutes when they told us to go to the auditorium. That was when I finally saw Darrell. He had been watching as buses brought in students.

Chairs had been arranged in circles in small groups of about ten. The room was filled with numerous authorities. There were a couple of women who introduced themselves as victim assistance counselors. They asked whom we were waiting to hear from and offered to help in any way. They stayed right by our sides. They began to ask many questions, and I broke down and started to cry. When they asked if they could call anyone for us, I said, "Yes, please call our pastor and his wife, Bruce and Claudia Porter of Celebration Church."

Some dear friends of mine came in and began to offer comfort and prayer. We went through an outside door and just cried together. A table was set up out there with cell phones. They offered me one so I could call my parents in Indiana. It was so hard to tell my mom and dad that Rachel might be a victim. Of course, their response was, "We will be on the next plane." My parents knew exactly what was happening to me and where I was emotionally because on two separate occasions, they had had a daughter and a son drown.

It was now dark outside. What had started as a beautiful, warm, sunny spring day had turned into every parent's worst nightmare. We were told there would be one last bus with remaining students. All the parents in the room were holding their breath hoping to see their children. As the bus emptied, my heart sank, and I fought off a wave of panic and total despair. Rachel was not on that bus.

A few minutes later, an announcement was made that missing persons reports were going to be handed out and that any children not accounted for needed to have a form filled out about them. When my eyes fell upon that form, all of the morning's precious memories filled my mind. I remembered exactly what Rachel was wearing, right down to my grandmother's silver wedding band that Rachel had asked to have.

I broke down, and my trembling hands couldn't write. Someone took the form from me and wrote what I told her to put down. I could still see in my mind's eye Rachel smiling, standing in my bathroom as she had just hours before, wearing a black tank top with a long-sleeved plaid shirt over it. Her pants were dark with a white stripe going down the side. Her hair was short with a red tint. Rachel had recently cut and dyed her hair to play a part in the school play. Her birth date was August 5, 1981. Somehow all of these details became very, very important.

Somewhere, from what seemed to be far off in the distance, I heard a voice on a PA system asking for our attention. The authorities collected the forms from us, but were giving out very little information. They were still not confirming any fatalities. They were, however, letting people know where injured students had been taken. Whatever hopes I had left were dashed when I realized that Rachel's name was not on any of those lists either.

After 8:00 P.M., we were told that no more information was going to be released that evening. We were encouraged to go home. No more information? Where was my Rachel? How could I just "go home" without my daughter? Was she alive? Was she wounded?

I knew in my heart that I needed to go home. I had four other children and a son-in-law there. Family members, our pastor, and others went with us to our house. As we drove up to our driveway, on the lawn sat my daughter Dana with friends, crying and comforting each other.

Inside Craig was sitting on the couch in a daze. I hugged him, but he did not seem to be aware of what was going on around him. Pastor Bruce and Claudia began to reach out to him. They were sitting beside him on the piano bench when the story of Craig's experience started gushing out. He was crying hard as he tried to explain what had happened.

Craig was in the library, sitting with Matt Kechter and Isaiah Shoels. The kids heard sounds like firecrackers going off. A teacher ran into the room yelling for the kids to get down, but until they saw a wounded student come in and collapse right inside the door, they thought that it must be senior pranks. Kids started crowding under tables. Craig was between Matt and Isaiah as they crouched together. Eric and

Dylan entered the room shouting and yelling. Craig heard one say, "Get anyone with a white hat." Craig had worn a white hat to school that day, so he quickly took it off and stuffed it inside his shirt. There was complete chaos as guns were going off, the alarms in the school were screeching, and the shooters were mocking and taunting their victims.

As Eric and Dylan approached the side of the library where Craig was, they spotted Isaiah, one of the few black students at Columbine. They made horrible racial remarks to him and shot him. But it was as if God put blinders on the killers when it came to Craig. Craig played dead so that he would not draw any attention to himself. They then shot and killed Matt before moving to another table. Craig had to lie there in the blood of his two friends who were lying dead on each side of him.

At some point, the shooters left the library. The roar of gunshots was so loud in Craig's ears that he thought his ears were bleeding. He could not tell the exact location of the killers, but he began to pray. Craig asked God for two things. First, he prayed for God to take away his fear, and second, he asked for courage. He felt God immediately answer his prayer, and his fear suddenly disappeared. He heard what he believed to be God's voice instructing him what to do next. He was to get up and get out and take everyone with him.

The kids were paralyzed with fear. Most of them were too afraid to move a muscle or say a word. Craig started rousing them, saying, "Come on! Let's get out of here!" One young lady who had been shot in the shoulder and was in serious condition was weakly calling out, "Please, please help me." Craig helped get her up, and with the other surviving students, they made their way out of a side exit door before the shooters reentered the library, intent on claiming more victims. Thanks to Craig's bravery, their remaining targets had escaped to safety.

That night was a painful, sleepless one. Craig was in complete shock and trauma, and brokenhearted sorrow gripped and overwhelmed the rest of the family. It was not until around 11:30 the next morning that we received a call from the coroner's office confirming that Rachel Joy Scott was among those who died on April 20, 1999. Even as I write these words, nearly a year later, tears stream down my face knowing that the destruction of that day cannot be reversed. Real violence has real consequences.

The following days are somewhat of a blur. We had to attend to the business at hand, arranging for Rachel's funeral and memorial service. My home was filled with people as family and friends poured in. The media, hopeful of gaining interviews with us, called constantly. Darrell and I were in agreement that all interviews would be on hold until after we had taken care of our daughter. We had to bury our dead.

Chapel Hill Mortuary offered its services and became a tremendous source of strength and help. A new product had just come on the market to serve families who had lost a child or young adult. Without hesitation, Darrell and I both knew it was for Rachel. It was a light beige casket that could be signed with a permanent marker. These tender expressions of love and farewell would be a part of Rachel forever. She had shared many little notes with her friends during her brief life, and we knew it would be something she would have loved.

Saturday, April 24, 1999, was chosen for Rachel's funeral service. We felt strongly that dwelling on the violence and horror of that awful Tuesday could not play a part of our remembering Rachel. She loved life far too much, and we would try our best to celebrate and remember all the wonderful things that made her so special to all of us.

That service came together because of the grace of God. I believe it was everything Rachel would have wanted. Rachel's love for people and for the Lord was obvious that Saturday. As members of her family and so many of her friends stood to give tearful tribute to her, we smiled, laughed, and wept over this wonderful gift she was to us.

The tributes expressed to my daughter brought great comfort and gladness to my heart; however, something even more awesome took place that day. I believe a supernatural phenomenon occurred during the memorial service. As our pastor, Bruce Porter, stood to speak, God inspired him to talk about a bloodstained torch that had fallen from Rachel's hand. He challenged everyone to take up Rachel's torch.

Only God knew how that moment would spark a generation of young people to take up the challenge of what Rachel and the other Columbine victims represented. We were later told that CNN, which televised her service uninterrupted, logged its largest viewing audience of any broadcast shown. It even eclipsed Princess Diana's funeral, which would have pleased Rachel greatly since she lightheartedly called herself "Queen Rachel."

Our family was the first to respond to that challenge of picking up the torch that Rachel and the other slain Christians at Columbine carried. In the following pages, we want to share with you the heart of a young girl who was totally given to pouring out her life for the Lord. Because her time on earth was cut short, we have committed ourselves to walking out her mission with the legacy of her writings, poetry, and artwork as a constant reminder of what this life is all about.

Darrell

A Father's Sorrow

At the time, I was working as a sales manager for a food company, and I also had a secondary hobby-type job that involved buying antiques and selling them at two different Denver-area antique outlets.

It was around noon, and I was at an antique outlet in Aurora, which is on the opposite side of town from Columbine. I had just begun unloading some items from my pickup truck when my cell phone rang. It was my fiancée, Sandy, on the line, asking me if I had seen what was happening on television. "There's been a shooting at Columbine," she said with a note of shock in her voice. That call was the beginning of what would be twenty-four hours of heart-pounding horror for me.

Even before the phone call ended I had goose bumps all over my body. I had two children at Columbine, my seventeen-year-old daughter Rachel and my sixteen-year-old son Craig, along with a nephew and a niece, Jeff and Sarah.

I dropped what I was doing, ran to the front of the outlet where I told the manager that I had to leave everything where it was, and jumped in my truck. As I rushed across town, I listened to a local radio station, which was giving sketchy accounts of multiple shootings and mayhem. There were no reports of fatalities yet, but the situation at Columbine sounded deadly serious. I could feel my heart pounding nearly out of my chest. I was terrified.

When I got about two miles away from the school, both lanes of traffic were jammed, and there was no way to get closer. Traffic became hopelessly gridlocked, and I was feeling increasingly agitated. I felt close to hyperventilating and hoped that I wouldn't have a heart attack right there in my truck.

I wanted desperately to be at the school and to know what was happening, but I was also fearful of what I might find out.

About that time there was an announcement on the radio telling parents to go to Leawood Elementary School, which is near Columbine.

Creeping along in the bumper-to-bumper traffic, I was praying for my children. For some reason, I wasn't concerned for Craig, but I was concerned for Rachel.

Craig was a big boy who was on the wrestling team. I guess I thought he could take care of himself. As I would find out later that evening, Craig had been in the school library between two boys who were shot to death, and he narrowly missed being killed. I believe his survival was a miracle.

My real concern was for Rachel, who was so feminine and so tiny. Maybe it is a father's natural instinct to want to nurture and protect his daughter and to assume that a son can take care of himself. That may be chauvinistic, but I wasn't analyzing things then. I was too busy navigating the traffic, hanging on to every word I heard over the radio, and praying to God for my children, my nephew, and my niece.

While I was praying, I sensed that God was trying to tell me something. I tried to hear His voice amid the confusion of my thoughts and feelings, but when I focused in, I heard these words again and again in my heart: *This is a spiritual event, a spiritual event*.

For the next thirty-five or forty minutes, I kept hearing the words: *This is a spiritual event*. It was almost as if I had heard a song on the radio and then couldn't get the melody out of my mind.

Chaos and Confusion

I finally arrived at Leawood Elementary School around one o'clock. It was a scene I will never forget. Hundreds of cars full of frightened parents had arrived before me, and I could feel my heart pounding once again. There was absolutely no place to park.

After what seemed like an eternity, I found a spot for my truck and half walked, half ran toward the school. One of the first people I encountered was my brother Larry Scott, who was running toward me.

"I don't know why, but I'm concerned about Rachel," I blurted out as soon as I saw him. Larry, a calm and comforting man who calls me Bubba, tried to help me relax. "Oh, Bubba," he said, "everything is going to be all right. They're bringing in kids by the busload right now."

As I looked toward the school, I could see a big yellow school bus pulling up with a load of kids who had been brought from Columbine. I also noticed that all around me were signs of both joy and sorrow. Here, parents hugged a child who had escaped from the tragedy unscathed. And there, a group of students sat together weeping.

I think I was experiencing something like preliminary shock. I was still covered with goose bumps and feeling a mixture of dread and disbelief about the whole scene. I kept thinking and hoping that maybe Rachel was hiding safely in the school somewhere, but I also was afraid for her.

The Long Wait

As I entered the pandemonium of the school, I was on my

cell phone talking to Larry Nimmo, the husband of Beth, Rachel's mother. Larry and Beth were at a nearby public library where, like me, they were desperately awaiting word about Rachel.

We talked throughout the day, promising to let each other know the minute we heard anything. Soon they called me with good news. Craig had called the house to report that he was okay. I was so relieved that Craig was safe, but my concern for Rachel only deepened. The long afternoon wore on. Busloads of kids continued to arrive at the school to be greeted by distraught but thankful parents.

I stood on my tiptoes, scrutinizing every bus for any sign of Rachel. Dozens of buses came, one after another, full of young passengers who were frantically hugged by anxious parents. And one after another, they drove off empty. As time passed, the number of parents waiting in the school became smaller and smaller. Later in the afternoon, school officials called all of us who were still waiting into the auditorium. I was growing more fearful for Rachel by the minute. I felt numb. And fewer buses were arriving at the school.

My worst fears worsened around three o'clock while I was standing outside the school. I happened to be near some young people who were talking and crying together. Amid this group I noticed one or two students who had performed with Rachel in the school play, which had been held a week or two earlier.

From a short distance away, I overheard one of them say the name *Rachel*. I edged closer, feeling as if my ears were giant radar dishes that could hear every syllable and every breath. Then one of them said she had seen Rachel's body outside the school.

I approached one of the boys in the group and asked him if

they had been talking about Rachel Scott. Looking at me with tears in his eyes, he said yes, they were.

I remember everything going into slow motion from that point on. There is a numbness that sets in that causes everything to seem unreal. All I could think to do was to call Sandy and let her know what I had heard. Sandy was working in her hair salon and had told me to call her as soon as I knew what was going on. She immediately left her clients and headed over to me.

As we would discover much later, a bullet had passed through Rachel's body and torn a hole in the covers of the journal she was carrying in her backpack.

THE COVERS OF
RACHEL'S JOURNAL

But I was still hoping against hope that what the young man had said was incorrect or that I had misunderstood him. During the rest of the day, I kept replaying what he had said in my mind, reexamining every word, and thinking that just maybe there was a possibility that it wasn't *my* Rachel he was talking about.

I was still holding on to some flickers of hope, but after a while, I became increasingly convinced that Rachel was dead. I don't think I could describe how I felt at that moment. More than anything, well, I guess I was absolutely stunned. I called Larry Nimmo on his cell phone and told him what I had heard, but I asked him not to tell Beth yet. I didn't want her to suffer needlessly if Rachel was still alive.

A Dwindling Crowd and Fading Hopes

Soon Sandy arrived, and I was able to break down for the first time and cry. She has been a tremendous source of comfort and strength for me during this time of grief in my life. By this time, Larry and Beth joined us with the rest of the parents waiting at Leawood. Their pastor, Bruce Porter, was with us too. While we were sitting there together in the auditorium, someone said he had seen Rachel on television among the wounded. We rushed to a television, but we didn't see any sign of her.

My emotions were on overload. In the course of a moment, I would go from total despair to anticipation to hope, all the while looking at every kid who got off those buses, hoping that the next person would be Rachel.

Then there was the announcement. The last busload of students from Columbine was on its way to Leawood. We ran outside, watching every young person step off that bus. I didn't see Rachel. My mind was playing all kinds of tricks on me, and I thought that maybe I had missed her. So I rushed back into the cafeteria to see if she was there.

When the last young man from the bus walked across the stage of the auditorium to be united with his parents, a handful of us were left. Looking around, I could see the members of the Shoels family, who were there with their aunts and uncles and cousins. I remember seeing the wife of Dave Sanders, who was one of the teachers at the school. And I remember seeing John Tomlin, who over the last year has become one of my closest friends as we have walked through this tragedy together.

All of us were there together in the auditorium, and I could see the glazed look on everyone's face. Some people were crying. Others seemed to be in shock.

I remember being in such pain that I could hardly think or talk. Sandy and I sat with our arms around each other for support. I was conscious of trained counselors in the room who were reaching out to the families, but I had not expressed a desire to talk with any of them. However, as we sat there I began to sense the presence of someone directly behind me. As that feeling grew stronger, I finally looked over my right shoulder. There sat a Catholic nun, praying silently to God with her hands stretched out to Sandy and me. There was something so serene and peaceful about her that I just turned around and spoke to her. She didn't say much, but her eyes spoke volumes. Sandy and I ended up in her embrace, and I remember just sobbing from the depths of my being. Looking back, I believe that was the moment when Rachel's death became real to me for the first time.

We stayed at the school until seven or eight o'clock that evening. People had brought in food, but nobody could eat anything. Sandy offered to stay up with me that night, but I declined. I went home to a sleepless night haunted by memories of a beautiful young girl who had been the joy of my life. I spoke her name thousands of times that night and wept until there was nothing but dry sobs. That night I could not see the positive impact her life and death would have on millions of people. All I could see was a huge hole in my future that could never be replaced. There are some things worse than physical torture or death. Losing a child is one of them.

Around eleven o'clock the next morning, I received the official call that Rachel was dead. She had been shot outside the school where she was sitting and eating lunch with a friend.

Media Madness

Soon all the people connected with Columbine found themselves at the center of a media cyclone. The media people treated me with the utmost sensitivity, but for the first month, I participated in interviews and media events in a dreamlike daze punctuated by painful moments of despair. Much of the time I was half expecting Rachel to walk through the door.

One particularly difficult time came while I was taping an episode of *Oprah*. Two years earlier, I had walked into my living room to find Rachel sitting and watching *Oprah*. She tilted her head, looked at me, and said, "Dad, someday you're going to see me on *Oprah*."

I had forgotten all about that moment until I was walking onto the sound stage and I looked up to see Rachel's photo on the screen. My knees buckled, and I fell to the floor.

Oprah came over to see if I was all right, and I shared that memory with her. She started crying. During the taping that day, we had to stop the cameras twelve times because people in the studio were breaking down and weeping.

Perhaps I was in a state of shock during those months. If so, I think that was God's gracious way of preserving me from totally falling apart.

My primary feeling during the whole period was an overwhelming inability to breathe. I really wanted to breathe. I felt that if only somehow I could take a deep enough breath, I would burst the whole oppressive bubble I was stuck under, and Rachel would be there with me again.

Over the next few months, I met and talked with people like Larry King, Tom Brokaw, Elton John, and President and Mrs. Clinton, but there was a numbness in everything I did. Nothing mattered to me at all, and it was as if everything in the world had the same bland vanilla taste.

Eventually the reality of the whole thing hit me. I would go to Rachel's grave and sob my guts out. I still visit her grave regularly. That's where I break down and cry. It is my point of release.

Beth

Surprising Discoveries

It would be months before Rachel's backpack was returned to us. The police were keeping it as evidence. One of the killers' bullets was in the backpack, where it had stopped after passing through her body and hitting her journal.

As I said, it would be several months before we saw this journal, but shortly after her funeral, other things she had written began to turn up. One of the first things I saw was a tribute Rachel had written to me. Over time, we found more writings, some in various journals and notebooks, and others written on single pieces of paper and placed throughout her room.

In a journal entry dated May 2, 1998, which was less than eleven months before the Columbine tragedy, Rachel wrote that it would be her last year of life. She wasn't fearful; she was thankful to God.

> May 2nd
> This will be my last year Lord.
> I have gotten what I can.
> Thank you.

In an undated journal entry, Rachel wrote out some verses about the brevity of her life.

> Just passing by
> Just coming thru
> Not staying long
> I always knew
> This home I have
> Will never last

As we struggled to deal with our grief over the next few months, we carefully examined what Rachel had written in her journals, in notebooks, in letters to friends, and everywhere else, including friends' high school yearbooks. What soon became apparent to us was that Rachel had a deeper spiritual life than we had ever known about, and that she seemed to have had distinct premonitions about her death.

Little by little, we developed a more complete picture of this young girl who seemed spiritually wise beyond her years.

Reading her letters to God and her friends, her poems and songs, her stories and prayers, we came to see that her spiritual insight was very, very deep. Sharing some of these insights is one of the main reasons we are writing this book.

Darrell

A Growing Understanding

After Rachel's death, we weren't eager to walk into her room, and we kept the door shut for a while. But over the next few months we found various journals full of her thoughts, books she had read, and pieces of paper she had written on, including one that was stuck underneath her bed.

We found a book that I had written years before. Rachel had studied it thoroughly, underlining and highlighting portions, and writing thought-provoking notes in the margins.

I had given a copy of the book to each of my five children, but on Rachel's I had written, "I can't imagine living without you." That is still the way I feel today.

A mixture of sorrow and joy filled me as I read my daughter's journals and notes, but along the way I came to a much deeper appreciation of her relationship with the Lord. I had known she had a relationship with God; I had no idea of the depth of her commitment and the utter sincerity of her spiritual walk. The last year has truly been a time of developing a growing understanding of her amazing interior life.

For both Beth and me, one of our regrets is that we never really understood how deeply she thought and how intense her spiritual side was. Now, in sharing her material with you, we hope that you will be half as inspired by her journey and experience as we have been.

2 "Living with the Lifemaker"

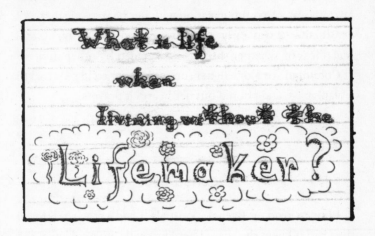

What is life when living without the Lifemaker?

For millennia, people wanting to draw near to God have sought Him out in silence and solitude.

Moses met God on a mountaintop. Jesus regularly retreated to lonely and quiet places where He could commune with His Father. And down through the ages, followers of Christ such as Saint Patrick and Saint Francis have received guidance, encouragement, wisdom, and love from the times they spent talking and listening to God.

Even Mother Teresa, a modern-day disciple who was best known for her tireless service in behalf of the poor, said she drew her strength from her private times of prayer.

Today, we live in a fast-paced and noisy world that beguiles us with its glittering images and lulls us with its omnipresent entertainment. Finding the time and the place for silence and solitude requires commitment and work.

For Rachel, the intimacy she desired with God typically came when she was writing in her journal, which was her favorite way of communicating with her heavenly Father.

Whether it was early in the morning or late at night, and regardless of whether she was surrounded by other students at Columbine or alone in her room, she opened her journal to a blank page and poured out her heartfelt prayers.

Beth

Opened Eyes

Prior to reading Rachel's journals, I had known she loved the Lord. I knew she shared her faith with others. I knew she was committed to her youth group and faithful in attending meetings. And I knew she was absolutely adamant about accepting people for who they were because that's what she believed God wanted her to do.

But these are all external things. Reading her journals gave me an entirely new perspective on the spiritual journey going on within Rachel's soul, much of which had been entirely invisible to me before. You could say that the journals opened my eyes to the inner spiritual life of my daughter.

What I learned surprised, amazed, and pleased me. The ongoing dialogue that went on in Rachel's soul between her and God wasn't like anything I had ever known before, and it certainly wasn't like my relationship with God.

Going Deeper

Rachel had always been a good girl in terms of her behavior and her morals. Outward goodness wasn't enough for her, however, and when she was quite young, she decided to go deeper in her walk with God.

When she was twelve years old, Rachel spent some time with relatives in Shreveport, Louisiana, where Darrell's father had once pastored a church. While attending a church service there, Rachel walked forward to the altar and prayed for God to fill her with the Holy Spirit. My sister-in-law, who told me the whole experience later, said it was a beautiful thing. Here is how Rachel later described it:

It was March 5, 1993. We went to their pentecostal church. They were having praise and worship and if you know anything about this religion, you know that they jump around and dance during praise and worship. I had always thought it looked funny till that night. Everyone was at the altar, and I felt so drawn to it. You have to understand that I was so young, and so for an twelve-year-old to be drawn that way, it was nothing short of God. I slowly walked up, till finally I reached the front. I sorta looked around and then closed my eyes and extended my hands toward heaven. I don't remember what I said, but I will never forget the feeling I had. That night, I accepted Jesus into my heart. I was saved.

Rachel came back from that trip with a noticeable change in her life. It's hard to describe precisely what the difference was, but she seemed much more spiritually attuned. I think that was the beginning of real spiritual awareness for her.

She had always kept little scrapbooks and notebooks around, and she would paste pictures in them, write notes to her friends, and do things to encourage others. But it seems that after her experience in Shreveport, her journals became a way for her to write about her growing relationship with God.

An Open Book

Rachel's pursuit of God was so intense at times. In one letter to God she wrote, "I'm sorry. I'm sorry I ever doubted you. I'm sorry I didn't trust you. You know what you're doing, and you know what's best for me. For now on, I put all faith and trust in you." After reading the things that Rachel wrote to the Lord and seeing how she talked so openly to God in her letters, I was either ashamed of myself or possibly convicted about how shallow my spiritual life had been.

In prayer after prayer after prayer, she would cry out to God in her writing and ask, "God, where are You? God, why can't I feel Your presence? God, why do I struggle?"

Some people are uncomfortable with that kind of frankness. They say that people should have faith instead of struggling with feelings like those. But some of the journal entries reminded me of some of David's writings in the Psalms.

At times, David was so overcome with the closeness of the presence of God that he could barely contain himself:

> Where can I go from your Spirit?
> Where can I flee from your presence? (Ps. 139:7)

But at other times, David felt the absence of God so strongly that he had to cry out:

> How long, O LORD? Will you forget me forever?
> How long will you hide your face from me?

How long must I wrestle with my thoughts
and every day have sorrow in my heart? (Ps. 13:1–2)

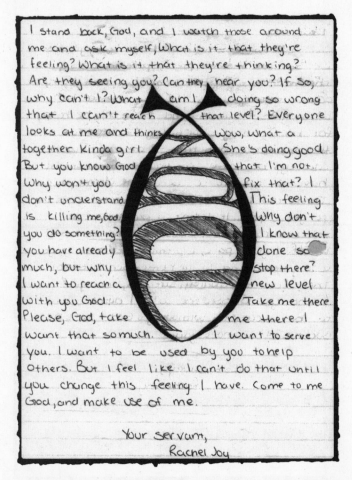

I stand back, God, and I watch those around me and ask myself, What is it that they're feeling? What is it that they're thinking? Are they seeing you? Can they hear you? If so, why can't I? What am I doing so wrong that I can't reach that level? Everyone looks at me and thinks wow, what a together kinda girl. She's doing good But you know God that I'm not. Why won't you fix that? I don't understand. This feeling is killing me, God. Why don't you do something? I know that you have already done so much, but why stop there? I want to reach a new level with you God Take me there. Please, God, take me there. I want that so much. I want to serve you. I want to be used by you to help others. But I feel like I can't do that until you change this feeling I have. Come to me God, and make use of me.

Your servant,
Rachel Joy

David talked to God about the very issues of his heart, and he was open and passionate with the Lord in his writings. And that is the same kind of sense I get when I read Rachel's journals. There is such a passion for God, such a transparency about her doubts and fears.

3/1/98

Dear God,

Sometimes, when I'm craving your Spirit, nothing happens. I stand there with my hands stretched towards Heaven, crying out your name, and nothing. Is it because I have not been keeping my quiet times? Is there sin in my life that is keeping me _____ from your salvation? What can ___ J E S U S ___ I do? Why have I been able _____ to keep faith like a child until now? Why do I have to _____ question your existance? I don't understand. I want to feel you in my heart, mind, soul, and life. I want heads to turn in the halls when I walk by. I want them to stare at me, watching and wanting the light you have put in me. I want You to overflow my cup with your Spirit. I want so much from you. I want you to use me to reach the unreached. I have such a desire and passion to serve, but I want to do that now I want to know and serve you now. I want heads to turn now I want faith like a child now. I want to feel you in my heart, mind, and soul now. I want you in my life now. I am crying out to you Father, asking for your spirit now. I thank you and love you for all the blessings in my life.

Your child,

Rachel Joy

Sometimes I camouflaged my emotions with religious words instead of being totally transparent with God about things. But Rachel was not afraid to put on paper the things that I would have been afraid to vocalize.

> Father,
>   I'm sorry. I'm sorry I ever doubted you. I'm sorry
> I didn't trust you. You know what your doing and
> you know what's best for me. For now
> on, I put all faith and trust in you
>   In Jesus Name,
>   Amen
>   Rachel Joy

I think her passionate intimacy with God went above and beyond what most people ever experience in their relationship with the Lord, but I don't think she thought of herself as a mystic or anything unusual. I'm not sure she understood the extent to which she had broken through the confines that too many of us allow to hold us back. But she was not confined. She had entered into a deeper experience of God.

Rachel had a powerful sense of pursuing something that she didn't know how to get a handle on, or how to grasp, or how to understand. She was looking for answers above and beyond the level that most teenagers would ever pursue. I think she was trying to understand God with an intensity that too many of us never seem to reach.

One thing is for sure, I don't think I'm a supernatural mother, and I don't think Darrell is a supernatural father. I took care of most of the physical needs of my children, I tried to help meet their emotional needs, and I tried to impart godly principles into their lives. I prayed with my kids, we had morning devotions together, and I organized family meetings so we could talk when things weren't going well.

But where would a child learn about that level of supernatural insight? I think the only explanation is that God led her to be that way.

Darrell

A Seeking Heart

Beth and I had joint custody of the children, and on weekends I would take them to church with me in Castle Rock, just south of the metro Denver area. When Rachel was twelve years old, she had a powerful spiritual encounter with God while visiting relatives in Shreveport, Louisiana. When she got back, she asked me if she could be baptized. She wanted to be baptized at the church in Castle Rock, Colorado, where I took the kids on the weekends. From that time on, we saw a depth begin to develop in Rachel that continued to grow until her death.

Rachel always had questions. I enjoyed being a teacher, so it was fulfilling for me to try to give her answers or to track down answers when I didn't have them.

One time when Rachel and the kids were young, they asked me, "Why does the moon follow the car?" I attempted to answer their question as best I could, but by the time I finished, they seemed more confused than before, and they were all looking at me and asking, "What are you talking about?" So I just said, "Because it wants to." Years later, I wrote a poem about that experience called "Why Does the Moon Follow the Car?"

That's an example of the kinds of things Rachel would ask about. She had a seeking heart and was full of curiosity about everything.

In the last couple of years before her death, her hunger for God and her desire to understand His ways grew more intense. During those years, she dared to ask questions that I believe kids should ask: Why does God allow evil? Or why did

He create the tree of the knowledge of good and evil if He knew humans would eat from it?

Over the years, we had some pretty deep Bible studies together, and we talked about things that went beyond typical Bible stories. Later, when I saw her journals, they filled me with tremendous joy because I saw reflected in her journals a lot of the concepts from the Bible studies we had done together.

Once she asked me to explain why the sun rose in the morning and why it set at night. I tried to explain that the idea of the sun setting and rising was an illusion. I told Rachel that the sun never really rose or set, but that it kept shining brightly all day long. From our perspective on earth, it looked like the sun was rising and setting as we circled around it. But that was just our perspective, and the truth was bigger than what we could see.

I must have done a better job explaining this than I did trying to explain why the moon followed the car because we got into a rather deep discussion about how we live in a world of illusion and many things are not the way they seem. We did a Bible study together about the difference between eternal things and transitory things, true things and false things. We talked about how the things we see are not to be trusted, but the things that are invisible are more real.

Sometime later, Rachel wrote about sunrise and sunset in her journal. In addition, there was a girl named Lindsay who had a class with Rachel two years before Rachel died. Lindsay said Rachel talked to her one day about the difference between real things and illusory things, and it was something that stuck in Lindsay's mind. "She made me think," Lindsay told me one day. "She planted seeds in my own thinking that have never gone away."

In a passage in a journal, Rachel used the metaphor of a camera to express her feelings about the visible world of matter and the invisible world of spirit. She concluded that her true essence could not be captured on film.

> Pictures
> Pictures of my life
> Everything captured
>   on endless black and white film
> Every moment, every angle, everyone
>   Where I am both the
>   photographer and the poser.
> Every sorrow, every laugh
> Every kiss, every hurt
> Censored to the public
>   Seen by my soul mates
> Captured by my hand
> Poised by my naked soul
> No... by my naked body
> For even the film
>   cannot capture my true form
>   My true existance

I loved Rachel's desire to plumb the depths of an issue, and I think her journals demonstrate that she wasn't content with a superficial understanding or existence. She wanted to go deeper into the reality of God and bypass what was transitory or illusory.

A Sense of Calling

Reading Rachel's journals, I wasn't surprised to learn that she had deep spiritual thoughts. Rather, I was surprised at how concisely she expressed some of the abstract thoughts and feelings.

I read these journals as if I were reading a book written by a stranger because they didn't seem like a teenager's journals, much less my own daughter's journals. The relationship with God I see revealed in her pages is not the norm for most people. Maybe it could be, but I am afraid it is not.

In my mind, I definitely consider her a mystic, which as I see it is someone who has a deep relationship with the Lord that transcends doctrinal or surface issues.

My spiritual heritage was one that included emotional exuberance in worship. However, I have come to realize that we can experience emotional feelings that become almost ritual in nature. Certain kinds of music can revive those feelings. Certain "trigger" words can program a response. One of the dangers of repetitive modes of worship is the possibility that we become a "sounding brass and a tinkling cymbal." In other words, we can perform without the substance being there.

In my own heart, I have prayed to be spiritual without being religious, to be able to walk in honest relationship with God that does not include "dead works" and the inclination to "perform" to impress others.

Rachel reached that point in her walk with God. She was incredibly honest in her diaries. She thought through the process of temptation on paper. She asked questions that some pastors never ask, much less teenagers.

The things that Rachel was expressing in her journals went way beyond religious clichés and all the preprogrammed modes we use to relate to God. She went beyond all this because she reflected honesty. You can see her struggles with faith and doubt on the pages themselves. On the same page where she would write about her deep conviction that God was in control, she would question whether God even existed.

In her writings, I see an emotional and spiritual depth, which shows that the things of God had penetrated her life instead of remaining on the surface.

Rumblings in the Soul

People do all kinds of things to get away from struggles in their lives. Some take pain relievers. Others drink or do drugs. Still others buy fancy cars or take expensive vacations in an effort to momentarily leave behind their troubled lives.

Something that surprised me about Rachel's journals was that there was pain in her life that I didn't know about. Even more surprising was the way she sought not to escape problems, but asked God to use them to teach her things.

Some of Rachel's pain was caused by the divorce Beth and I went through. She writes of the tearing that she felt, the sense of conflicting loyalties between her mom and her dad, and the feelings of abandonment she experienced.

In addition, she expressed the sadness she experienced after being rejected by friends at school. Sometimes people who were otherwise very close to her made fun of her because of her faith in God, and their comments hurt her very deeply.

Instead of trying to deaden the suffering or turn away from her God, she acknowledged it, learned from it, and asked God to walk through it with her.

A Passion for God

Rachel had a holy passion that at times consumed her. That doesn't mean she was a fanatic, and she would never hit people over the head with a Bible. But she was brutally honest with herself, and she had an unbridled passion to serve God.

Today, young people may not see a lot of examples of this kind of dedication in the people around them. But perhaps Rachel can be an inspiration for someone who wants to know what an intimate and honest relationship with God looks like.

Willing to Submit

I think Rachel understood that being a Christian and taking up the cross mean that we lay down our need for control, giving the control up to God. She saw that Christianity meant submitting. She knew that God's grace touches us most deeply when we are weak, not when we are strong.

The question I see on page after page of Rachel's journal is this one: Who's in charge of things, us or God? It's a question we all need to ask ourselves.

God,

    Where are you? What should I do?
JESUS, I call upon your name?
Deliver me from my ways.

       RACHEL

3 Flawed but Faithful

RACHEL AS
A TODDLER

In the weeks and months after the Columbine killings, Cassie Bernall, Rachel Scott, and others were hailed as modern-day martyrs or national heroes because of their combination of fortitude and faith under fire. There was an unconfirmed rumor going around that the girls were being considered for canonization.

But Rachel and the others were no saints, at least if what you mean by saint is the stereotypical image many people have of a near perfect person who never sins and hovers a few feet above our fallible and fallen world. On the other hand, if a saint is someone who is faithful to God even amid failures and doubts, then perhaps Rachel qualifies.

No matter what you call her, Rachel's deep faith—and the passion and sincerity with which she pursued her relationship with God—is something we can all learn from.

Beth

A Good Girl

As a mother, I have to say Rachel was a very good girl who caused me very few real problems. Usually she was pleasant in her personality, and she had a quick wit, which always helped her to see the funny side of situations. Those attributes help a person survive difficulties.

On the other hand, she wasn't perfect. Whether she was right or wrong about something, she was very intense in whatever she did, and that occasionally led to stubbornness on her part. She could also be melodramatic or charm her way into getting what she wanted.

There were times when Rachel gave me a quick answer that revealed a disobedient attitude. And like any regular kid, she routinely fussed and fought with her siblings. As the middle of five children, rather than be the forgotten child, Rachel used that position to her advantage and was quite independent. She did not exactly fit in with her older sisters, Bethanee and Dana, or her younger brothers, Craig and Michael. By the time Rachel was three years old, she already had two baby brothers. Actually she was pushed out of her babyhood very quickly. I believe she learned at a very young age how to be her own individual.

My daughter was not a superhuman saint, and I think she probably would have been a little exasperated to be categorized that way. To her, trying to be perfect wasn't being real. One of Rachel's strongest passions was to be very real about who she was, and it would have frustrated her to have someone put her up on a pedestal. She would have tried to crawl off the pedestal and plant her feet on the ground again.

Seeking Self-Esteem

Today, young people face tremendous pressures while growing up. Our culture places a very heavy emphasis on physical appearance. Rachel, too, had struggles with self-esteem, even though it seemed that many of them had been resolved in the year or two before her death.

Rachel struggled with her imperfections. She had a conviction that she needed a nose job! Rachel had fallen and broken her nose when she was young, and the accident left a little bump on her nose. I didn't think it detracted from her looks at all, but she was very self-conscious about it and always wanted to have it fixed. The family teased her about it quite often, and she usually joined in the fun. The family always considered her to be the beauty.

The fact that someone like Rachel had doubts about her appearance proves how difficult it is for young girls growing up today to have confidence about who they are and how they look.

Rachel knew she wasn't perfect, and you can see from reading her journals that she valued honesty. She wanted people to be honest with her about her faults. She hated pretension and dishonesty, and she much preferred to have people tell her what bugged them about her rather than hide it and pretend everything was okay.

Likewise, she wanted to be honest with God about her doubts. Instead of trying to conceal them or cover them up, she let her doubts and anxieties come out in the pages of her journals.

From the outside looking in, it may appear to some people that Rachel's self-esteem was based on her looks, her personality,

October 15, 98

Jesus, break these strongholds
Tear down the strings of sin
Release me from my pride
Rescue me from these games
Restore me from the hurt
Renew my heart again
Tear down this bondage
Destroy this burden
Give me love, Give me peace.
My life, my love, my wants
My needs, my passion,
My strength, my faults,
My sin, my friends,
My foes, my family,
My all... is now yours.

her talents, or something external like that. But if you really knew her, you would know that the source of her self-esteem was something much deeper.

She knew God made her, and she knew God loved her. This knowledge helped make her well grounded. I think that one reason she struggled so much in her letters to God and in her prayers was that she was afraid of not being able to be true to herself. She wanted to be faithful to God, and she wanted to stand for what she believed in.

> Dear God,
>   Haven't talked to you in awhile. I guess I've just given up. I don't know why, but it's getting to be too hard. Each day, I play the question, "Do you exist," over and over in my mind. I know you do... but even with the fact of your being, I have a hard time believing. I'm so confused... I don't know what to do. Where do you want me? What do you want? I want to be used in great ways... but I haven't the courage nor the strength. Help me through this stage of pain, through the hurt and thru the rain

She was aware of how often she failed to be faithful to God, but she did not get frustrated and give up; her flaws helped her remain humble before God and dependent on Him for her sense of balance and satisfaction.

Facing Temptation

Temptations seem to be everywhere for kids today, and Rachel faced temptations on a daily basis. I know she struggled with smoking because she told me about her temptations in this area.

Probably a month or two before she died, Rachel came to Larry and me and said, "I need to talk to you." She seemed very serious and apologetic, and as we sat down to talk to her, she said, "Mom, I've done two things that you're not going to be proud of me for. But I want you to hear it from me, not from anyone else."

The first thing she told us was that she had recently gotten a speeding ticket. As a mother, I'm a little protective. Rachel was a good driver, but she wasn't all that focused. So I told her that she couldn't travel on Interstate 70 or Interstate 25, two major highways that go through Denver. Rachel especially wanted to be allowed to drive on I-25 so that she could drive herself to youth group meetings. So one night Larry and I decided to let her drive, and we rode along to see how she handled herself. By the time we got to the church, Larry and I were wrecks. It had been all we could do to keep silent about her driving skills.

Then one night Rachel and some friends drove to Lookout Mountain, which is north of town, and getting there requires driving on I-70. While she was driving, she got a ticket for speeding. I have always prayed that my kids will get caught whenever they do something wrong so that they know there are consequences for making wrong choices. That time, my prayers were answered very directly. I know Rachel came to us because she struggled with feelings of guilt when she disobeyed us, and it was on her conscience.

The second thing we learned was that she also smoked cigarettes for a while. She told us, "I want you to know that I have done this, but I'm not going to be doing it anymore." She confessed that she had succumbed to pressure because she had wanted to be a part of the group.

The Opposite Sex

Only after her death did I learn about Rachel's struggles with sexual temptation. In this, too, she was brutally honest with herself and with God, even though such honesty wasn't easy.

Rachel had a boyfriend she really cared for a great deal, and in time she became concerned about where the relationship might develop physically. She was scared to think that she might trespass her deeply held moral standards and ideas of sexual purity.

What did she do? She gave up her boyfriend. She literally walked away from the one young man she probably loved because she didn't want the relationship to turn her away from who she was called to be. It was tough for her, and she wrote about her struggle in her journals.

Rachel's temptations were not that much different from what a lot of young people are faced with these days. The way she handled them was not to trust herself but to commit all her ways to the Lord.

As I said before, Rachel would have trouble thinking that people were holding her up as a sinless saint. But if she thought her transparency about her shortcomings and doubts could inspire others to be more honest with God, she would be glad to serve as a role model.

Darrell

Who's Perfect?

I agree with Beth. Rachel would find it incredibly humorous if anyone ever called her a saint. She would be flattered, but I can just picture her laughing at that. Rachel didn't think of herself as a saint because she was too familiar with her human weaknesses.

It would not be wishful thinking for me to say that in many ways, Rachel was above normal. I have five children, and she required the least maintenance of them all. When the other four children read this, they'll know what I mean, and they'll understand.

But she had faults and flaws, and she never pretended to be perfect. As Beth pointed out, Rachel was never happy with her physical appearance, and she and the family joked about it. She was blind to her own beauty, and I think that helped people of all kinds, shapes, and sizes relate to her.

She also struggled with the typical petty jealousies, and she wrote about that in her journal. In one instance, she wrote about her conflicting emotions after another Columbine student got a lead role in a play.

That is the kind of thing Rachel worked on, and during the last years of her life, I never heard her say anything negative about anyone, even though she had been severely mistreated by some of her closest friends when she became more serious about her commitment to "walk her talk."

Rachel worried that she fell short creatively. She was involved in plays and drama at school, but her acting didn't come easily for her, and she worked hard at what she did. She attempted to create artwork, but she was very frustrated because she felt she wasn't good at it. I have a painting she drew for me that I hung up on the wall for a while, but later she laughed about it because she viewed it as "a child's art." Meanwhile, her sister Dana is an incredibly good artist. Rachel could see the difference. Rachel tried to write songs and poetry, but she got upset because her poetry didn't rhyme. I always thought her poetry was better than my own.

In all these things, she never viewed herself as having reached her goals or accomplished what she set out to do.

I can see a certain sense of frustration in her writings. She

3/2/98

Dear God,

I know that at first I was really jealouse
of   She's sweet, pretty, popular, & she got
the major part for the drama. But now I only
admire those qualities. You have blessed her
with gifts & talents and I can only be happy
for her. Thank you for giving her lead role in
the drama. It has taught me that I won't
always be in the spotlight. I am thankful to
have a chance to be in the drama at all.
Tommorrow I have an audition. I am not expecting
to get a part. If I don't, I promise not to
critize or become jealous of those who make
[   ] If I get a part, I promise not to let it go
to my head, and I will remember to thank
Thee, for the ability, strength, courage, &
talent you blessed me with. I don't want
to be successful without you God. I can't be
successful without you.

Love always,
Rachel Joy

felt that she was nowhere near where she wanted to be. And
yet she learned to be herself, particularly during the last two
years of her life. When I read her journals, I see her struggles,
but I also see her sense of contentment with who she was.

One of the Bible studies I did with Rachel was about perfection. We talked about how God is perfect, but people are
flawed and fallen. In the end, I don't think Rachel believed that
she was supposed to be perfect. Rather, she knew that the God
she served is perfect. That's an important distinction, and it
was something she thoroughly understood.

Struggling to keep the candle burning
Enemies surround me blowing their cold breath,
Hoping to extinguish the flame
My candle, lit be the last of my matches, is subtle, but it is their
Eating out the last strand of wick
Melting the last drop of wax
Then... darkness, alone
Laughter, wicked laughter, screams in my ear
The coldness rips at my skin
Depriving me of my heat
I breathe in the emptiness around me
Taking it in as air, but choking as if it were smoke,
Smoke blackening me within
&t is no longer the darkness around me
That torchures and destroys my flesh
It is the darkness within
That destroys what once
was sacred
The destruction feeds on my soul
The hatred burned in my heart
The lies upon my tongue
The hurt flowing through my fingers
Morals lost, and sins gained
Lost, forever lost.

"Go and Sin No More"

After Rachel's death, I found out that she had experimented some with smoking. Although she had stopped shortly before she died, it was clear that she went through the usual temptations that young people struggle with today.

She also wrote about struggling with the temptations to go out with friends she knew would be drinking. She cared about these people, and she wanted to be with them, but she didn't want to do everything they did. So she wrote about the whole progress of temptation, the various rationalizations people can make, and how she dealt with it all. I was overwhelmed as I read about her struggles with peer pressure and watched her temptation unfold on paper, how she thought through the situations and made her choices.

Rachel had a much better understanding of God's grace and sovereignty than I did at her age. Although I was raised in a Christian home, I think that my early years were more an

April 15, 98

Dear God,

I promise that I will not drink this Friday when I go out with _____ This is so tempting. I want to go so bad. Well, I thought about it (as you know) and I thought that since you would forgive me anyways I may as well do it. Then I realized that you will always, always forgive, but you may not let it go unpunished. Then I decided not to do it strictly out of fear. Then I thought about it more, and thought that if I did it out of fear

> it would not be done because
> I loved you, I obeyed you, and
> I followed you. That is my
> reason for not going now.
> I know that I will always
> be faced with temptation,
> but because I love you, I
> obey you, and I follow you,
> I will not fall into the core
> of it. Thank you, Father
>   ☺always
>   Your child,
>   Rachel Joy

attempt to obey rules and regulations to earn my salvation than a walk of faith. The reason is I misunderstood God's ways.

Jesus constantly warned His disciples to "beware of the leaven of the Pharisees." He was talking about legalistic rules and regulations that seem to be good but actually produce nothing but self-righteousness. That is the deadly trap of legalism. In Colossians 2:20–23, Paul warned Christians that commandments and teachings of men such as "Do not handle! Do not taste! Do not touch!" project an appearance of holiness but do nothing to actually produce grace or holiness in our lives. Rachel had come to understand the difference between spiritual principles and legalistic rules and regulations. It is such a thrill to see your own children respond to the grace of God.

One of Rachel's favorite Bible studies that we did together was about the difference between the seed and the sod. I had helped her to understand that we were made from dirt and our bodies will return to dirt. However, that dirt is the planting ground for an eternal seed. Farmers don't look for clean dirt when they plant seeds. They don't vacuum all the dirt out of the garden so the seeds won't get dirty. They need the dirt for the seed to grow. In fact, sometimes the dirt isn't dirty enough, so they spread cow manure over the dirt to make it dirtier! They call this rich soil.

When we focus our eyes on "self," we're looking at the dirt. When we focus on the seed growing in the dirt, we produce fruit! It is so important to understand that the Christian walk is not me becoming perfect; it's Christ growing to perfection in me. There are two verses that sound contradictory in the Bible, and yet they form a complete truth: "I can of mine own self do nothing," and "I can do all things through Christ which strengtheneth me."

Rachel knew the difference between the seed and the sod. She knew that once the seed began to grow, people would no longer look at the dirt, but instead focus on the emerging fruit of that seed. She knew she wasn't perfect. But she realized that God was doing some wonderful things within her.

Time Is Short

Rachel had an inward motivation to accomplish as much as possible. She sensed an urgency that she often wrote about. We now realize that there was a spiritual awareness on her part that time was short. She talked about the fact that she would not live long enough to get married. She wrote several poems that showed her awareness that she would die young.

Her death has caused me to consider the remaining years of my life. I was on an airplane recently that developed major engine problems, and we were forced to make an emergency landing. I found that there was no fear in my heart through that whole experience. I have also been made aware of the brevity of life and the need to walk out each day as though it could be my last.

Ten months after the Columbine tragedy, two young people were murdered in the same Subway shop where Rachel had worked. She knew both of them. The young man had drawn a picture of Rachel and given it to our family after her death. The young woman lived in a house directly behind Rachel's bedroom, less than fifty yards away. If Rachel had not died at Columbine, she would have probably been at the Subway shop that night. She wrote in one of her poems, "Tomorrow is not a promise—but a chance." The lives and deaths of all these precious people should challenge us to live life to its full potential every day.

4 Finding Hope in a Broken World

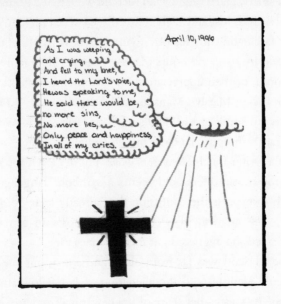

In the days after the Columbine tragedy, pundits and commentators reacted with shock and surprise. Many of them asked, How could something like this happen in a prosperous, peaceful, and supposedly happy place like Littleton, Colorado?

Meanwhile, Internet chat rooms became havens for hundreds of people who expressed a different view of the tragedy. There, in the safety and anonymity of virtual space, young people from around the country said they understood the alienation and anger of the two killers.

"I know how they feel," wrote one on-line author. "Parents need to realize that a kid is not overreacting all the time when they say no one accepts them. Also, all of the popular conformists need to learn to accept everyone else."

Though few American teens are probably as angry and hate

filled as Eric Harris and Dylan Klebold were that day, many are apparently as lost and alienated as these two were. Many share their fascination for historic figures such as Adolf Hitler, or their desire to spend hours playing violent video games such as Doom, or their appreciation for extreme musicians such as shock rocker Marilyn Manson or industrial rockers KMFDM. Harris put some of KMFDM's nihilistic lyrics on his Web site: "If I had a shotgun, I'd blow myself to hell."

As a writer for the *New York Times* put it, "Even the rawest extreme music offers adolescents a symbolic language with which to express the confusion they already feel. Communicating the anguish of victims and outcasts in a voice of vengeance and aggression, it theatricalizes rage."

Rachel Scott was far from bitter and angry, but she could certainly identify with the alienation of her fellow students, and she had tasted her share of the heartbreak and brokenness of life.

When Rachel was around seven years old, her parents—Darrell Scott and Beth Nimmo—separated and later divorced. Although they are reluctant to talk about these matters, both parents realize their failures had an impact on their children.

Darrell

Failure and Forgiveness

I am responsible for my part of a failed marriage. I went through several rough years of introspection and self-abasement until I realized that I needed God's grace to forgive others and myself as well. Thank God for His gracious forgiveness and cleansing power. I had taught other people that

God was a Mender of broken vessels, and now I had to submit to my own teachings and allow that to happen in my life.

Regardless of the reasons for a divorce, it is never easy when children are involved. Children will always be affected by divorce. They need their parents more than ever after a family has been torn apart. If you are the divorced parent of children, please understand that God wants to use you to bring healing to your children. Do not try to heal your own hurts by encouraging your children to choose sides or by bad-mouthing your ex-spouse. That will only damage your children, who will one day resent you for it.

I knew the importance of both a mother and a father image for children. I made a decision to never say anything negative to my children about their mother. They needed her, and they also needed me. We had joint custody of the children, so I had them with me every weekend. As they got older, they would sometimes spend more time with their friends, which was understandable.

Beth and I were able to resolve our conflicts several years before Rachel's death. I am grateful for that because things would have been so much harder if we hadn't. There are many Christian divorced families, and I want to encourage you to let God bring reconciliation to your family. Broken homes can be healed. They may remain split families, but there do not have to be unforgiveness, bitterness, and strife.

Both Beth and I are now remarried. I am saddened by the fact that Rachel died just before Sandy and I were to be married. She had written in her diary that her dad had met a wonderful lady with three awesome sons. She had grown to really love Sandy and constantly asked me, "Dad, when are you and Sandy getting married?"

On January 30, 2000, Sandy and I were married. The first thing we did after the ceremony was take the whole wedding party out to the cemetery where Sandy placed her bouquet on Rachel's grave.

Beth

A Family Falls Apart

From the time I was a little girl, I was raised to believe that marriage and family were sacred responsibilities, so when Darrell and I separated in 1989, my whole world fell apart. Out of fear and desperation, I became a woman of prayer as I never had before. With any divorce situation that includes children, there is great pain. Our children were no different; they each suffered in their own way. They really missed their dad!

During all of this emotional upheaval, I had to start thinking of a way to contribute to the financial support of five children. I used to joke and say, "There just isn't any demand in the job market for an ex-pastor's wife." Having been raised in a pastor's home, I knew nothing but working in ministry. Now I was taken from being an in-the-home full-time mom to being a caregiver and helping provide for the family financially. This was a huge challenge, but little by little God helped me make good decisions.

I regret that Darrell and I did not resolve our issues as husband and wife, but I am grateful that we had resolved most of the problems long before April 20, 1999. I can't imagine what it would have been like to lose Rachel and have hard feelings still between us. I am thankful for the touch of God that forgives and brings healing.

Depending on God

As I said, prayer became like an obsession to me. There was an urgency in my heart to constantly feel the love of God. I prayed for two things every day. First, I prayed that my children would be safe and that I would know how to care for them in every way. I had taken Darrell for granted in so many of the business areas of life that I had very little experience. Second, I prayed for the healing of my own heart. I was very broken and felt personal failure and low self-esteem.

God was good to me during that time. I felt that God became my husband. I developed a deeper relationship with the Lord than I had ever experienced before. It was at this point that I started including my children in daily morning prayer.

Every day during our devotional time we shared our requests, and many times the kids would pray for something. We were well aware that it was God who was taking care of us and meeting our needs.

A year after Darrell moved out, my parents helped me buy a home in Columbine. This really was God's provision because I did not even have a steady job. During the first two and a half years of separation, I worked doing odd jobs here and there as I could find them. The children experienced all of this with me. I was finally offered a job that would enable me to learn accounting skills.

As Rachel observed all of this transition, she started making little jokes about never getting married. When she was young, she never played house or pretended to get married, and she wasn't one to play with dolls very much.

For the last several years of her life, Rachel referred to herself as "Queen Rachel." She loved to carry herself in a royal manner, which of course included being waited on by other family members. At one point, our telephone answering machine greeted callers with this message: "Hello. You have reached the house of Queen Rachel and her servants Larry, Beth, Dana, Craig, and Michael. If you have anything you want them to do for me, please leave a message."

Such antics didn't offend Rachel's siblings. Her sister Bethanee fondly remembers even her tendency to be dramatic:

God shared a piece of heaven with me for seventeen years, and I will treasure my memories with Rachel in a special place in my heart reserved only for her.

Rachel,

I miss you with all my heart. More than I can express. I miss your smile and laughter. I miss playing the piano with you. I miss hearing your voice, especially when you were being dramatic. All I want is to have you back with us again. Everyone around you was affected by your joy and energy. Your hopes and ambitions were so contagious. Just to see you again for an instant would be worth all I have.

Sometimes my heart feels non-existent, except for the pain it holds that lets me know my heart is still there. My mind races constantly to keep all our memories fresh and unfading. Each one is golden and priceless.

Now when I close my eyes, I am with you. I can see your face, and you smile with me again. Your smile brightened mine. Tears flow down my face as I picture you in your bridesmaid dress, as I see you perform your mime in the high school talent show, as I see you in the living room watching a movie.

In all those places, I am with you longing to hold you, in all of them. Your touch will always be a treasure.

Even from heaven you have continued to give yourself to us thru all your writings and journals. You could not have left us anything more precious.

Thank you, Rachel! And thank you, God.

Love, Bethanee

A large part of her Queen Rachel persona included *no cooking!* Rachel could not cook at all. Once Larry asked her to peel some potatoes and put them on to cook so we could make mashed potatoes. Well, she peeled them, put them whole into the pan without water, and turned on the stove. Thankfully Larry came in the kitchen a short time later. He could not believe that Rachel did not know how to boil potatoes. But it didn't bother Rachel. Her philosophy was, she would marry a rich man and hire a chef. Why waste time doing something like peeling potatoes? When Rachel made tossed salad, the result looked like she put a whole head of lettuce in a bowl, threw in a tomato, and—voilà—tossed salad. Rachel was faithful to help with chores—*if* they didn't include cooking.

Queen Rachel did have her low moments when she did not feel or act like royalty. Those were the times when she would struggle with her fears and doubts, and she would question God.

However, Rachel had a resiliency that allowed her to see the sunshine after the clouds disappeared. Most of the time, she would come right back with an "up" attitude and be her perky little self again.

There is a portion of Rachel's life that in some ways escapes me. So much of my focus was on taking care of the everyday responsibilities that Rachel grew up in some areas before I

As emotions shift,
Decisions drift
As confusion clouds
Unsureness bounds
All things are hazed, distorted, & out of focus
My heart is numb, twisted, and broken
   How can I give
   How can I receive
   Nothing can be asked
   Or given to me

knew it. Because Rachel did not demand a lot of attention, I spent more time tending to the needs of my children who were the "squeaky wheels." During this period, Rachel was

Dec. 14, 96

You said "that's bad"
I said "so what"
You said "He lies"
I said "He's fun"
You said "Please stop"
I said "Shut up"
You said "I love you"
I said "Not now"
But then the matches
Burned my hands,
And he was not there,
To care for me,
He left me,
In the dark alone,
But I was not alone,
You said, "I love you,"
I said, "Why"
You said, "Because I made you"

becoming more and more intimate and private. The dialogues she had with the Lord demonstrate her comfortableness with Him. God was becoming a beloved Partner she trusted and depended on. The conversation with God at the bottom of page 60 shows her debating back and forth until it becomes clear that He loves her.

From June 1989 to November 1995, I was a single parent. My children and I adjusted our lives the best we were able. When I met Larry Nimmo in the fall of 1994, I was not thinking about marriage at all. Larry and I started dating, and our relationship developed into so much more. It was a joke between us that only a crazy man would marry a woman with five teenagers in the house. During our dating period, my children gave Larry a hard time. They would "charge" him money to talk with me on the phone. Bethanee and Rachel were especially great at this. Bethanee always teased Larry about seeing him on *America's Most Wanted*, and I think as far as Rachel was concerned, Larry probably owed her one or two million dollars for being allowed to talk with me.

After our marriage, our family again started going through major adjustments. Larry had only one son, and he had moved to be with his mother. My oldest son, Craig, had been the man of the house for all of those years, so for him the adjustment was especially difficult. We faced some hard times in trying to find balance in our new roles. Rachel loved Larry, and for the most part, they worked well together to have a good and healthy relationship.

However, with all of the change and adjustment, there were tension and frustration in the home, and everyone was trying to cope. Rachel once again responded by taking all of these problems to the Lord.

> January 21st, 98
>
> Dear God,
>
> I ask for your help in this household. I ask that you replace the hate, with your love. I ask that you soften hearts, open eyes, and silence tongues. I ask that we come together not just as a family, but a family in Christ. I thank you for each member and I thank you for each blessing that will come upon them. I rebuke Satan in the name of Jesus. I bind him from this family
>
> Amen

Darrell

A Father's Final Talk

A few days before Rachel died, she and I had one of the best conversations we had had in years. I didn't know it then, but that would be our last real talk.

Rachel had been out late one night and was cited for breaking the Littleton curfew, so I had to take her downtown to pay a fine. She hadn't done anything wrong, but the city is strict about its curfew, and she had violated it.

Afterward, we were sitting at my dining room table. We

didn't purposely sit down to have a heart-to-heart talk. We just started talking, and suddenly I found myself saying things that surprised me. I realized that I was in the middle of a father-daughter conversation with someone who once was a little girl but had gradually become a big girl. Graduation was still a year away for Rachel, but I began sharing with her about all kinds of things.

I talked about how I hadn't always been a perfect dad. I told her that I tried to do the best I could, but that I was sorry we hadn't spent as much time together as I had wanted to.

I talked about how Sandy and I were looking forward to having grandchildren, and my whole life I had been preparing to be a grandpa. We laughed about that together, but she always got quiet when we talked about her having children or even getting married. I think part of that was her premonition that she wasn't going to be around long enough to be married.

SANDY, DARRELL, AND RACHEL

As we talked, I told her that I loved her unconditionally. I remember saying that if Rachel or any of the other kids ever had children, I would love the grandchildren regardless of whether they were black, green, purple, orange, or any other color. I told her that I would love them if they were gay or anything else.

"I can't imagine not loving my grandkids," I said. "And for me to be able to say that about grandkids who don't even exist yet, how much more do you think I love you, Rachel?"

A few days earlier I had lunch with two longtime friends that Rachel knew. "We poured our hearts out to each other after not having seen each other for years," I told her. "I have an unconditional love for those two guys, who were such a part of my life, but they couldn't ever mean as much to me as you do."

Rachel had a unique way of tilting her head to the side when she was thinking seriously, and she was doing that during this talk. And I remember her beautiful smile.

Our conversation was intense. By the time we finished, we were both crying. She got up and came around toward where I was sitting at the table, and I got up and met her at the head of the table. We hugged and sobbed together.

I didn't know at the time that it was to be our good-bye talk, but looking back on it now, I know there was nothing left unsaid between us. It was a total openness, and I believe that God ordained that talk.

Months after Rachel had died, somebody asked me what I would want to say to her if she could come back. I thought about it and answered like this: "I said everything I had to say to Rachel that day. I told her exactly how I felt about her, and I told her how much I loved her. We left nothing unsaid. We left no stones unturned."

I never would have expected that Rachel would be taken from me only a few days later, but I thank God that we had such a heartfelt talk together.

God Uses Broken Things

In America today when something breaks, we typically throw it out rather than fix it. People have called ours a disposable society.

I'm thankful that God doesn't do things that way. Our entire world has been broken ever since the Fall, but He hasn't given up on the human race yet. God lovingly works with broken people to restore and redeem them, using the cracks in their lives to create something beautiful.

The day after the Columbine killings, Jonathan and Stephen Cohen, two brothers who attended the school, wrote a song about the tragedy called "Friend of Mine." They sang the song at the April 24 Columbine Memorial Service, which was attended by an estimated seventy thousand people and was broadcast live by CNN to a worldwide viewing audience.

One of the things that makes the song so powerful is the Cohens' affirmation that God can bring hope out of horror:

Can you still hear raging guns ending dreams of precious ones.
In God's son, hope will come, his red stain will take our pain.

The song's final lines promise that peace will come out of heartbreak:

Columbine, rose blood red, heartbreak overflows my head.
Columbine, friend of mine.
Peace will come to you in time.
Columbine, friend of mine.

Rachel was aware of her brokenness, but she was also

aware that God was working in her to make her whole and complete.

In one of the many songs she wrote, she described her sense of worthlessness, contrasting that with her deep conviction of God's loving work in her life. All of us need to understand this message. Sorrow and failure—even on the grand scale of Columbine—are not the end. They are simply a new beginning for God's redeeming grace.

Break me of my pride, Oh God,
Tear down my string of sins,
This life of filth and worthlessness,
Unto You I willingly give.
Take it from me, all of it,
Do with it what You will.
Take me and mold me God,
Your foundation, begin to build.

chorus

My life has brought *me* only shame,
~~But~~ through it Your Will ~~is~~ *be* done,
What once was sorrow and endless blame,
~~Is~~ now the start of things to come.
My story now a testimony,
A thing nothing short of God,
I keep His Name forever holy,
For my life, with His blood, is bought.

chorus 2x's

5 Love from Above

When I feel,
Your powerful presence,
I fall to my knees,
And cry in repentance,
All I feel,
Is your wonderful love,
And this only comes,
From Heaven above.

Private grief became national mourning on Saturday, April 24, 1999, when the nearly three thousand people who gathered in Littleton's Trinity Christian Center for the funeral of Rachel Scott were joined by reporters from the international news media and cameras from cable network CNN, which broadcast the service to millions of viewers.

Sorrow at Rachel's passing mixed with joy about her memorable zest for living as one after another of her friends stood up to share stories and anecdotes about her brief life.

"Rachel was small in stature, but she lived big," said Barry Paulser of Orchard Road Christian Center.

Her life was big as a Christian in her school at Columbine. At the talent show recently, while others were performing mimes

67

and dramas on the things of this earth, Rachel was performing things about heaven above. When others were ignoring and even talking and making fun of students who didn't fit in, Rachel was trying to reach out to them. She was fearless in her faith, and although it may have been offensive to some, she just kept on letting her little light shine.

The many reporters covering the event strove to capture its emotional power and its impact on the people who were there.

"They lined up next to the pulpit, aside the white coffin covered with the felt-tipped signatures and farewell wishes that will be buried with her. And one by one, they told Littleton and the world the story of her life," wrote Associated Press reporter David Foster, whose account of the funeral was published in dozens of newspapers.

"Friends remembered a young woman who lived up to her middle name, Joy, and whose passion for life, for people and for her religion inspired those around her," wrote Laura Berman of the *Detroit News*.

Sacramento Bee writer Gary Delsohn focused on Rachel's brother Craig and the other members of her immediate family, who did not speak during the service:

Brother and sister, they have come to symbolize the awful tragedy of Columbine High School. One died, the other lived.

With Craig Scott and his devastated family sitting in the front row at Trinity Christian Center, 3,000 people joined them Saturday to mourn, and celebrate the life of Rachel Joy Scott.

And Bill Duryea, a reporter for the *St. Petersburg Times*, described some of the brief memorials that friends wrote on

Rachel's casket, which was kept closed during the funeral service, but was opened afterward.

"Rachel, sweetie, I love you," wrote one. "Can't wait to see ya again. Have fun in my father's house. I wish you were here, but you're in a better place. P.S. Jesus, please take care of her."

Another friend wrote the following: "Rachel, you were an example of the love of Jesus to me. Your actions + dedication to Christ have truly changed the world."

You will be reading other eulogies of Rachel, but if you can, try not to think of them as tributes to one possibly exceptional young woman. Rather, think of Rachel's life as an example of the amazing things that can happen when any of us, no matter how ordinary, open our hearts to God's deep and boundless love.

Darrell

A Love for God's Creatures

If you've ever read anything about Saint Francis of Assisi, you know that he loved people, animals, nature, and just about everything else God had made. Rachel was the same way.

Everyone who knew her knows that whenever she was out walking, she had a history of taking the time to stop along the way and say, "Oh, look at that flower." Sometimes people who were with her would get frustrated and say, "Oh, come on, let's keep moving." But she was constantly doing things like that. She had the habit of stopping to smell the roses, as they say.

If she was out somewhere and a puppy dog or a cat walked by, she couldn't resist stopping to pet him or rub his tummy. At the shopping mall, she had to stop to talk to little babies. I loved to watch her with babies. She would get down on her hands and knees so she could be on their level and just love on them, and they loved her too. She always took the time to appreciate all of God's creatures, which, as Francis said, are recurring signs of God's grace and love for us.

Standing Up for the Underdog

Don't get me wrong. Rachel's love wasn't merely a sentimental thing. Her love for God's creatures didn't stop with flowers, puppies, and babies.

Whenever she sensed an injustice being done to someone, no matter how small or seemingly insignificant it was, righteous indignation rose up within her.

She grew up with two brothers and two sisters: fighting and arguing among them all were not unusual. But sometimes when her brothers got in a particularly contentious argument, she acted as a referee, trying to decide who was being mistreated and doing what she could to correct it. She had that instinct built into her.

Rachel even served as my conscience sometimes. I don't savor talking about this, but I think it helps understand the way she was.

Rachel at times brought conviction to my life in the area of compassion toward others. She was always ready to stand up for anyone who she felt was mistreated. I grew up in Louisiana at a time in our history when there were total segregation and much prejudice. I never considered myself a racist, but I picked up a certain amount of unwanted baggage along the way. I am thankful that my children didn't grow up in an environment where hatred toward others was encouraged.

I can remember times when I would be with Rachel and I would make a remark about a guy on the side of the road who looked totally healthy with a sign asking for money. She would always rebuke me and want to stop to give something to help. The world is a much better place because of people like Rachel Joy Scott.

Rachel was very sensitive to the underdog. She had a tender heart toward people rejected by others. Shortly after the Columbine tragedy I talked with a mother of one of the slightly wounded victims about her son. She told me that he had been born with a physical disability that caused him to talk slowly and also affected his appearance. Other students would make fun of him and shove him around at school. However, Rachel went out of her way to find him in the halls daily just to speak a few words of encouragement.

Later, at a professional softball tournament featuring the Denver Broncos, Nuggets, Avalanche, and Colorado Rockies, I sat behind this young man in the bleachers. He told me that several hours before Rachel died, she had put her arm around his shoulder and told him she was going to buy him lunch in a few days and wanted to know all about his family. With tears in his eyes he looked at me and said, "Mr. Scott, nobody has ever been as kind to me as your daughter was. I really miss her." I vowed, then and there, that as I traveled around the country speaking to massive groups of young people, I would share his story and challenge them to start a chain reaction of acts of kindness in Rachel's honor.

The Story of the Gloves

Among all the things we found after Rachel's death, there

was a story she wrote that captures her compassion for the underdog. It is called "Gloves of Conviction." I don't think she wrote it for a class at school. I don't even think she wrote it for anybody else to read. Rather, it was something she wrote out of her heart after failing to care for somebody as she felt she should have.

The story is about a needy-looking woman who came into the Subway sandwich shop where Rachel worked. I think we have all been in similar situations, and typically many of us prefer to turn away and mind our own business rather than reach out to someone who obviously looks as if she could use our help.

For Rachel, this one episode of failing to help someone who was more vulnerable than she was troubled her deeply and inspired her to write this story. I hope it moves you to a deeper experience of compassion for others.

Gloves of Conviction

I was opening that day for work. On Sundays, no other employees come in until 11:00, which meant I had two hours of work to do by myself and then open the store for another hour alone with customers.

Usually no one comes in until about 11:30 on a Sunday morning anyway, so I always have plenty of time on my hands. I couldn't believe how windy and cloudy it was. The cold of the breeze alone could bring you to a chill.

It was 10:00 so I flipped the switch for the open sign and unlocked the doors. It must have only been five minutes after that when I heard the doorbell ringing, telling me I had a customer. I went out front and began to put the gloves on, ready to make the first sandwich of the day.

I looked up and saw a woman who must have been in her late forties. She was wearing several layers of clothes. They were torn and dirty. Her face was dark from dirt. She was shivering, and then she began to cough in an almost uncontrollable manner. She looked up at me after she was all right and she gave me such a warm smile.

"What can I do for you, Ma'am?" I asked.

She looked at me pleasantly and said, "Oh, I was just wondering if you happen to know what time the busses were coming. I have been waiting out in the cold for two hours. You think they wouldn't be so late, especially on a Saturday."

I felt bad when I told her it was actually Sunday. She looked at me with such embarrassment and shock.

"Oh no," she said. "I need to get back down town. I thought it was Saturday. Do you mind if I just sit here for a while until I figure out what to do?"

I told her no problem, and she sat at the table in the far corner. As I looked at her and the situation more carefully, I realized she must have been so poor, and maybe even homeless. She was dressed in the dingiest clothes that hadn't been washed in a while. She had a snug, winter hat on, three layers of flannel, baggy pants, worn-through tennis shoes, and gloves. Her gloves were turned inside out. They had fringes coming off all sides.

I felt right then and there that I should have made her a sandwich free of charge. Then I should talk to her, telling her that whatever she did, God loved her and wanted her to trust him and fall into his arms once again. I knew where all of this was coming from. I knew God was giving me these words and asking me to go talk to her. But what if . . . what if . . . the usual questions and doubts about why I shouldn't.

I went back to work, trying to forget about it, and hoping she would leave soon. My next customer came about an hour after that. She was a woman in her early thirties. She was well dressed in what looked like a work outfit. She had her hair pulled up nicely, and she was laced with perfume.

I made her some sandwiches, and we were at the cash register when she asked me how long the other woman had been sitting there. I told her about an hour.

"Did she get anything to eat?" the lady asked me.

I said no, and told her about the busses. Then the lady asked me if I wouldn't mind making one more sandwich. I looked at her and smiled.

I never made a sandwich with such happiness and at the same time guilt. I told the lady no charge, and handed her a bag of chips to go with it. She thanked me and then went to the other woman.

She handed her the food and began to talk to her. They must have talked for two hours before I saw them leave. As I was cleaning the tables and feeling bad for not talking to the woman myself, I noticed that she had left her gloves.

I told God that I was sorry for disobeying him. He told me something that will always give me a boldness in these situations, something that will never make me hesitate to tell others of him:

"You feel like she missed something because you lost your boldness, but she didn't lose her opportunity. The other woman is sharing with her right now and she will not lose out on me.

"You lost. You passed up the chance to gain something. You just let a wonderful flame go past you and into the hands of another. Let this be known, child, when you do not follow through with the boldness and knowledge I have given you, more than one person is affected by it. You are as well as they."

Darrell

A Life of Love

Like all people, particularly young people, Rachel struggled with issues of self-esteem and tried to find her place in the world. She wasn't overpowered by these feelings, as some people seem to be, but she felt their sting on a regular basis.

And as I mentioned earlier in this book, I believe that when her mother and I separated and divorced, Rachel's sense of insecurity increased. The two people who should have been there for her more than anyone else couldn't keep their marriage together. This affected her in ways that I will probably never fully understand.

In her journals, Rachel often wrote about her yearning for love. Entries like the one she entitled "Dreaming . . ." make it sound as if her yearning remained unfulfilled.

Dreaming...

I close my eyes
I open my mind
I think of things
Yet to come
One day I will see
The face of my love
One day I will be
In somebody's arms
Until that day
Will come to be
I close my eyes
And dream a dream.

Everyone has struggles with sorrow and disappointments in life, but I think the thing that makes the difference is what we do about them next. How do we respond to our struggles? What do we do about the pain and brokenness in our own lives?

By talking to Rachel before she died and reading her journals after she was gone, I have become convinced that Rachel took the vast majority of her problems to God and left them in His infinite care. It is kind of like leaving your case in the hands of a jury or a judge. Rachel would go to God and make her case, then she would leave the decision in God's hands.

As you can see from her journals, Rachel had an extremely intimate relationship with God. I don't believe her relationship was any deeper than yours or mine *could* be, but somehow it *was* deeper than most I have seen over the years.

I think this intimacy with God is the key that unlocks the mystery of who Rachel was and how she could be so loving to everyone she met and knew. It's as if her heart was filled to overflowing with the love of God, and this love flowed out from her and touched others too.

At times, it is hard to tell if the companionship Rachel cries out for in her journal is human or divine. In one entry, the two kinds of love seem to be interwoven.

Am I the only one who sees
Am I the only one who craves your glory
Am I the only one who longs
To be forever in Your loving arms
All I want is for someone to walk with me
Through these halls of a tragedy
Please give me a loving friend
Who will carry your name, until the end
Someone who longs to be with you
Someone who will stay forever true

But Rachel didn't wait until her romantic love needs were fulfilled before she followed God's command to love others. She seems to have received love directly from God, and this love gave her the strength to love others.

Something that jumped out at me from her journals was that Rachel really understood she was not the issue; Christ was. She realized it was okay for her to be weak because she knew weakness is where God's strength is made perfect in all of us.

I would like to share some more of the things that people said about Rachel at her funeral, but please understand me. My goal is not to build her up as if she was something extraordinary. Rather, I want you to see how all of us—no matter how torn and troubled we are—can be vehicles for God's supernatural love and compassion.

Memories of a God-Centered Girl

I'll never forget all the people who spoke at Rachel's funeral and all of the wonderful things they said. Let me share some of their comments with you. I think they will illustrate the various ways Rachel sought to share God's love with people.

RACHEL
GOES FISHING

Pastor Lori Johnson was Rachel's youth pastor:

What I wanted to say about Rachel was that she was an amazing, amazing girl. She had this fun, full-of-life side where she had so much energy and made people laugh. She would wear these crazy hats sometimes, and dress in crazy ways just to be different. She was never afraid of being her own person. That's what she wanted to be, and I always admired the strength that she had.

She also had this really deep thoughtful side. She would write poetry, and she cared so much about people. Through it all, there was a passion and a love that she had for God and for people that consumed her life and consumed everything about her.

Rachel had two dreams: she wanted to make an impact for God and she wanted to live in His presence all the time. It's amazing to me that God has fulfilled both in her death. I love you, Rachel. I'll see you in heaven someday.

Mark Bodiford was a young man Rachel had reached out to and befriended from her church's youth group.

I haven't had the best life, and I've always prayed to God that he would send somebody who would love me, who would care about me, and who would make me feel wanted. I just praise God for sending me an angel. In the short time that we had our friendship, Rachel made me feel like the most important person in this world. She called me her bigger brother, and I just say this to you, Rachel: I love you, and I know you're in heaven, and I'll see you there someday.

Nick Baumgart took Rachel to Columbine's prom the Saturday before the Tuesday shootings.

Rachel was my friend, and a truer friend you couldn't find. Her name, Rachel Joy Scott, is perfect right in the middle there. Joy was what she brought to everybody she ever met. Whether you knew her or not, it didn't matter, she still brought it to you.

Also, her trueness to herself was amazing. She didn't let anybody affect who she was. She didn't let anybody tell her that what she believed and who she was wasn't okay. She was true to herself, and because of that, she was true to everybody else. In a sense, she still is here. She always will be, and that smile will always be here. You know, you could be having the worst day of your entire life and all she had to do was smile. I'm lucky to have known her, I'm fortunate to have been her friend, and I'm fortunate to have called her my prom date. But I'm truly blessed to have had her in my life.

Sergio Gonzales had been a friend of Rachel's since the fourth grade.

We met the first day of class, and she shined back then too. Here's just one quick story.

I remember one Halloween. I wore a Zorro costume to school, and I hated it because my mom made it and I felt pretty dorky. And Rachel came to me and said, "What's wrong with you, Serge? I love Zorro. I like him. I'd like to be him. You wanna switch costumes with me?" And ever since then, we just had this bond that grew and grew ever since our first play in fourth grade and until our last play that we just performed at Columbine.

I know Rachel loved life because life was just like one big amusement park to Rachel, and a glorification to God. She always told me to love life and not worry so much about the little things. She was the kind of person who would tell me, "Serge, you need to get over it." She taught me that more than anybody else, and I'll always remember her.

Brianna Cook was someone Rachel reached out to at school.

What I remember most about Rachel is when I first came to Columbine, I didn't fit in or anything, and Rachel was the first person who ever came up to me and opened her heart to me and brought me in.

My car always died and we'd always go to Subway to find Rachel and she'd always jump my car. It was the little things like that that always meant a lot to me, and she always put her feelings aside and put other people's feelings up front. She wrote me a lot of poetry that means a lot to me. I love her.

Andrew Robinson was assigned to be Rachel's mentor in forensics and drama. He wrote the play that Rachel starred in weeks before the shooting.

My name is Andrew Robinson, but to Rachel I was just Robinson. I was assigned to her early on to be her mentor. Pretty much everybody who had me as a mentor wanted to be reassigned, because I have kind of a reputation for not being very nice, I guess. On the first day, when I told her she could be reassigned to someone else if she acted quickly, she looked at me and said, "I can take anything you can dish out and then some. So bring it." And I said, "Okay, we're going to bring it."

I've never met a finer young woman with such drive and goals, and I always thought that when I left Columbine it was in good hands because she was right there keeping step with me. I really thank her for that. She reaffirmed my belief that there really are truly, truly, truly good people.

RACHEL'S
GRAVE SITE

Sarah Scott was one of Rachel's cousins and a close friend.

Rachel was the most incredible, passionate person I've ever met in my life. We grew up together, and we went through so much together. Before she passed away, she was at my house, and she took my yearbook, and she wrote some stuff in there. I'd like to share what she said in my yearbook, because it will stay with me forever:

"It's hard to find God through these halls, doubt is a part of every man's journey, but don't lose faith." And that's a message to everyone at Columbine, because God is in our halls, you just have to find him.

Another thing she wrote to me was: "Sarah, don't let your character change color with your environment. Find who you are and let it stay in its true colors."

The night she died, I wrote a poem about her. It's called "Angel of Mine."

> Looking down, seeing despair
> Only leaving a soul searching for air
> Feeling the warmth, seeing the light
> Reaching for wings for the eternal flight
> Slipping away from this world today
> Angel of mine you've found your way.
> Let my love be the wind beneath your wing
> As you rejoice in heaven and sing.
> Angel of mine
> Your face will make the heavens so bright
> With your beauty, grace, and loving spirit.

Only God knows why Rachel was shot, but I know I shall never forget my beloved friend and cousin, Rachel Joy Scott.

After Rachel's friends sat down, Pastor Billy Epperhart said,

One of the poignant things that was said here today was about Rachel's ability to get along with anybody, and her ability to understand people and other kids where they were.

Instead of trying to fit into a group or trying to fit in somewhere, she just fit in everywhere and related to people where they were. Her brother and sisters and her cousins shared the fact that you could tell her anything and she wouldn't condemn you, she wouldn't beat you up.

I believe it was the love that Rachel received from God that allowed her to be so strong and loving to many others.

Searching for Security and Significance

Every human being has two tremendous needs: the universal needs for security and significance. Rachel and I used to talk about these things and study together to see what the Bible said about them. By understanding what we talked about, I think you can have a better grasp of the source of Rachel's love and strength.

Security, which includes our basic survival-type needs for food, drink, and shelter, is our first need. If we're not secure, nothing else matters. People don't worry about significance when they're wondering about where they're going to get their next meal or sleep that night.

Significance is less about physical survival and more about our emotional needs for being esteemed and appreciated. Once we've dealt with our security issues, we start dealing with our significance issues. We ask questions about how we can be fulfilled, how we can find our place in the world, and what we are supposed to do with our lives. I believe that God has built into all of us a desire to make a difference in the world and to accomplish something for others.

When Rachel and I would talk about this, I asked her to get out her Bible and mark every place in the text where it said that we are "in Christ" or "in Christ Jesus," and then to go back through with another color and mark every place where it says "Christ in you" or passages like the ones in John talking about Christ "abiding in you."

My point was that true security and true significance can come only from understanding what it means to be "in Christ Jesus" and what it means when it says, "Christ in you." Our security comes from understanding our position in Christ and all that is provided there. Our significance comes as we "decrease" and allow Him to "increase." His life, lived through us, brings fulfillment. As Paul wrote, "It is not I, but Christ who lives in me."

Security comes from understanding what it means to be in Christ, and significance comes from understanding that the Christian walk is not me being somebody. It's not me being famous. It's not me being great. It's Jesus being Himself in me.

Too many people try to find security and significance in too many places. They look in relationships; they look in popularity; they look in money and possessions. But these are all detours and dead ends. Our true security and significance are found only in Christ, and I believe Rachel knew that.

Seeking and Finding a Friend

Rachel wrote much about friendship in her journals. One entry describes what a true friend is. Maybe this would be a good model for all of us to follow in our relationships with others.

a friend...
A friend is someone who can
look into your eyes and be able
to tell if your alright or not
a friend...
a friend is someone who can
say something to you
without you telling them
anything and their words hit
the spot
a friend...
a friend is someone who can
brighten your day with a simple
smile when others try to do it
with a 1,000 words ~~the~~
a friend...
a friend is someone who can
reach out their hand
and help you thru the hurt
a friend...
a friend is someone who can
help me talk to me the way you
do... and in you I have
found a friend

6 The Call to Commitment

Over a period of years, Columbine killers Eric Harris and Dylan Klebold recycled their own hurts and hatreds until their souls were filled with a simmering rage at the world.

As students at Columbine High School, the two angry young men didn't respond outwardly to the perceived slights they received at the hands of fellow students, but they internalized their alienation, amplifying it with violent video games such as Doom and music by shock rocker Marilyn Manson to produce fantasies of bloody revenge.

After the killings, parents of their victims heard rumors that Harris and Klebold had made videos about their murderous plans, but in the months following the tragedy, no one saw the tapes or reported on their contents.

But that all changed after a reporter for *Time* magazine got access to the tapes, and the twenty-page story he wrote about what he saw appeared in the weekly news publication just before Christmas 1999. The magazine featured a controversial cover photo taken by a Columbine security camera showing Harris and Klebold in the midst of their shooting spree.

The exhaustive story explored the damaged psyches of the two killers, including their anger at blacks, Jews, and athletes, and their desire for celebrity, a craving that led them to speculate whether filmmaker Steven Spielberg would consider directing the movie about their lives and deaths.

Missing Motives

Curiously the reporter overlooked one important aspect of the killers' motives. Darrell Scott and Larry Nimmo (Rachel's stepfather) immediately noticed the omission when they and other parents watched some of the tapes. Numerous comments the killers made on their grisly premassacre videos made it clear that they shared an intense anti-Christian hostility.

"What would Jesus do?" asks Klebold at one point in the tapes, making fun of the popular WWJD slogan that appears on more than a million bracelets and T-shirts. Yelling and making faces at the camera, Klebold asks a second question. "What would I do?" he screams before pointing an imaginary shotgun at the camera, taking aim, and making a shooting motion and corresponding sound: *"Boosh!"*

In the same tape, made on March 15, Harris is heard saying, "Yeah, I love Jesus. I love Jesus. Shut the f*** up." Harris later chants, "Go Romans. . . . Thank God they crucified that a******." Then the two troubled teenagers join together in chanting, "Go Romans! Go Romans! Yeah! Whooh!"

All this was troubling enough for Darrell Scott, who could bear to listen to only one of the killers' five videotapes. But then he heard Klebold, who had reportedly had a crush on Rachel, single her out for particular disdain, calling her a "godly whore" and a "stuck-up little b****."

Clearly the two Columbine killers meant to wreak as much death and destruction on as many people as possible on that April 20. Their grand design called for using nearly one hundred explosive devices.

According to a Littleton Fire Department report issued in February 2000, Harris and Klebold created 49 carbon dioxide or "cricket" bombs, 27 pipe bombs, 11 propane gas bombs using 1 1/2-gallon tanks, 7 incendiary devices using more than 40 gallons each of flammable liquid, and 2 bombs they carried into the school in duffel bags, each using a 20-pound gas tank. If more than a few of these devices had worked, it is possible that hundreds of Columbine students would have died that day.

When the mass executions failed to happen as designed, Harris and Klebold resorted to killing students one by one, and a surprisingly large number of their victims were committed Christians.

The fact that the killers had used religion as a criterion for selecting some of their victims was discussed as early as April 22, two days after the shootings, by three reporters for the *Washington Post,* who wrote a story with the headline "In Choosing Victims, Gunmen Showed Their Prejudice." That story included these two stunning paragraphs:

While investigators here continued today to sift through the aftermath of the rampage for clues to the shooters' motive, relatives and friends of several of the slain students said that they believe some victims were targeted because they represented all that Eric Harris and Dylan Klebold disdained.

There is no evidence that the murderous pair moved through the corridors with a hit list of names. But it was widely known among Columbine students that the tiny subculture to which Harris and Klebold belonged had little tolerance for devout Christians, or for athletes who favored caps, or for the handful of minority students who attended the school.

Who Said Yes?

In the days and weeks after the killings, Columbine victim Cassie Bernall, who had dabbled in witchcraft and discussed murdering her own parents before she experienced a dramatic Christian conversion, became an inspiring symbol of courage and commitment for millions of young people across the country.

Cassie's legend grew even more after the publication of her mother's brave and moving book, *She Said Yes,* and after a music video of Christian singer Michael W. Smith's song "This Is Your Time" was dedicated to her memory.

According to stories that first circulated immediately after the tragedy, Harris and Klebold asked Cassie, who was studying in Columbine's library, if she believed in God. When she answered yes, she was shot in the head at near point-blank range.

"Because of her last words, Cassie Bernall is now being hailed . . . as an authentic martyr for the faith," noted an article in *Newsweek*. A writer for the *Boston Globe* said, "In her death, Cassie has become both symbol and prophet."

Later, there was debate in the media about whether or not Cassie had been the person who publicly confessed her faith and died a martyr's death. Apparently the surviving student who claimed he heard Cassie say yes later grew confused about his account. Such confusion would be understandable amid the chaos of the shootings and the trauma of the aftermath.

As the debate continued, other students came forward to suggest that the student who was actually asked if she believed was Valeen Schnurr, another of Columbine's many committed Christians. She was injured—but not killed—in the library that day.

Rachel's Final Moments

Meanwhile, friends and family of Rachel Scott were hearing accounts of her final moments. Most of the stories were attributed to Richard Castaldo, the young man who was eating lunch with Rachel outside the Columbine library that fateful morning.

Richard, who was shot more than half a dozen times and remains paralyzed, has problems retrieving memories of that day, but during a January 2000 taping for a segment of NBC's *Dateline* newsmagazine, Richard's mother confirmed that she had heard her son describe Rachel's death in the initial days after the tragedy.

According to Richard's earliest account, he and Rachel were sitting outside when they saw Harris and Klebold approaching. Without warning, the two young men opened fire, severing Richard's spine and shooting Rachel twice in her legs and once in her torso.

As Richard lay stunned and Rachel attempted to crawl to

safety, the shooters began to walk away, only to return seconds later. At that point, Harris reportedly grabbed Rachel by her hair, held her head up, and asked her the question: "Do you believe in God?"

"You know I do," replied Rachel.

"Then go be with Him," responded Harris before shooting her in the head.

When it's all said and done, the precise details of the Columbine students' deaths make little difference. As Misty Bernall, Cassie's mother, wrote in *She Said Yes,* "The world looks at Cassie's 'yes' of April 20, but we need to look at the daily 'yes' she said day after day, month after month, before giving that final answer."

Rachel's parents feel the same way.

Beth

Living—and Possibly Dying—for God

I have many reasons to believe Richard Castaldo's account. While NBC was taping a segment on Rachel, Richard's mother came forward and documented that Richard had initially said that Rachel was asked about her faith. But Richard has locked down that day in his mind now. He can no longer recall what happened. He has blocked it out of his memory, which has happened a lot with kids who survived this tragedy.

There's absolutely no doubt in my mind that Rachel died the way Richard first described it, but it doesn't really make any difference to me or her family members because we were aware of her deep commitment to Christ long ago.

Rachel's decision to perform a Christian mime to the Ray

Boltz song "Watch the Lamb" in the annual school talent show clearly demonstrates her commitment to God. Many of the students saw the talent show as an opportunity to do something fun or silly, but Rachel saw it as a wonderful opportunity to perform mimes to Christian songs with a real message.

I think she was definitely going against the grain in doing this, and there were always a few mockers in the crowd. But she was not worried about criticism or ridicule. I know that she was walking a line that was not popular, and it cost her in being ridiculed by certain groups of kids. She knew she would take some heat for being that up front about her commitment, but she was willing to pay the cost.

In Rachel's case, it wasn't a sudden outburst of courage that allowed her to perform the explicitly Christian mime and risk the ridicule of her friends. Instead, it was a consistent approach to putting her happiness last on her list of priorities.

That approach can be seen in a journal entry addressed to her cousin Jeff.

> May 4, 98
>
> Jeff
> - only a month left of school. If you had to make a list of the top 5 things most important to you, what would you put? Here's mine.
>
> 1. God
> 2. Family
> 3. friends
> 4. my future
> 5. myself
>
> always,
>
> Rachel Joy

Rachel performed another mime in the 1998 talent show. As Rachel started her performance, the audiotape sound became very garbled, and the music stopped. The audience started looking around to see what was wrong. Meanwhile on stage, Rachel kept right on with her mime. It was probably at least two minutes before the tape was fixed and the music came back on. Since Rachel had been keeping the song going in her head, when the tape restarted, she was in perfect step. She was miming the Ray Boltz song "The Hammer." It is about a Roman soldier who witnesses Jesus' crucifixion and asks the question, "Who would nail this innocent man on a cross?" In the song, he comes to realize it was his own sin and the sins of the world that crucified Jesus. Ironically Dylan Klebold was in the sound booth that night, and he was the one who eventually fixed the audiotape. Once again, through Rachel, the gospel had gone forth even to her killer.

As Rachel left the stage, the audience applauded her for her bravery in not abandoning her performance. Darrell had been working late but was trying to get there in time to see Rachel's part. He did not make it until she was walking off the stage. His timing was perfect. Rachel was crying and felt totally humiliated as she walked past the curtains, and who was standing there but her father? Dana and I rushed out of the auditorium to be with her backstage. We all comforted her, and only a few minutes later she stopped crying and resolved, "Well, next time I will make sure that my tape won't fail me. I will be better prepared. I have learned a hard lesson but one I will never forget." She lifted her head, and that was that.

Rachel was very committed to Christ. She wasn't a middle-of-the-road person. She wasn't apathetic. She had a vitality for life and an all-out devotion to what she considered important, and that devotion seemed to come through in even the smallest things that she did.

Rachel had love and concern for family members who were experiencing difficult times. Her cousin, Daniel Cecrle of Shreveport, Louisiana, has suffered tremendous pain and affliction since his birth. Doctors are amazed that Daniel is still with us. Rachel wrote a prayer asking the Lord to intervene on his behalf.

She also prayed and wrote notes of encouragement to another cousin who was struggling in so many areas of his life. One note said:

> You wanna know what I feel—what I think about constantly—that is on my heart . . . GOD. Seriously, He is all I think about. I want to serve Him so much . . . So sorry if I came on so strong. I just wish you knew how it feels. I just feel so happy and fulfilled. I know that you don't understand right now, but I'm praying that someday you will . . . You are one of the most important people in my life, that's why I want to give so much of God to you. Just to have Him in my life has made such a difference.

I could see some of this in her while she was alive, but I have learned much more from others after her death. I have heard testimony again and again about kids she witnessed to, outcasts she talked to, needy friends who would call her late at night and talk to her for hours on the phone, and lonely people she loved and reached out to. Many students that we never knew before have come forth and told us about her commitment. Such testimonies only confirm some of the things she wrote in her journals about putting herself last. I believe that was what she tried to do much of the time.

Counting the Cost

A lengthy journal entry demonstrates how far Rachel would go to honor her commitment to Christ. I call this her "Dear Sam" letter. It was something she wrote to a friend on April 20, 1998, which was exactly one year before the Columbine killings.

The letter described how she had been dumped by five of her closest friends after she decided to get more serious about living out her faith.

> April 20, 98
>
> Dear Sam,
>
> It's like I have a heavy heart and this burden upon my back... but I don't know what it is. There is something in me that makes me want to cry... and I don't even know what it is. Things have definetly changed. Last week was so hard... besides missing Breakthru... I lost all of my friends at school. Now that I have begun to walk my talk, they make fun of me. I don't even know what I have done. I don't really have to say anything, and they turn me away. I have no more personal friends at school. But you know what... it's all worth it

to me. I am not going to apoligize for speaking the Name of Jesus, I am not going to justify my faith to them, and I am not going to hide the light that God has put into me. If I have to sacrafice everything... I will. I will take it. If my friends have to become my enemies for me to be with my best friend Jesus, then that's fine with me. Ya know, I always knew that part of being a Christian is having enemies... but I never thought that my "friends" were going to be those enemies. It's all good, I'm just a loner now at school. I just wish that someone from Breakthru went to my school.

Always in Christ,

Rachel Joy

It's obvious that her decision to do what she felt was God's will cost her dearly. She talked about how she lost five friends, friends who were in the church and were part of her youth group. They literally turned their backs on her because she decided to "walk her talk." The names of the girls are not important, but the way they treated Rachel shows how difficult it can be for someone to be a committed Christian in today's schools and even some churches.

Rachel was the kind of person who could have had much popularity at school, but she wasn't one to pursue that. She wanted to be a real friend to all kinds of people more than having superficial popularity or shallow relationships with the "popular" students. She did things unconventionally. She walked away from the privileged circles in order to reach out to students who were lonely or sad or hurting in some way.

She was walking her talk, and I think Rachel paid the price in the way that some of her so-called friends excluded her.

Faithful but Not Fanatical

I knew something of Rachel's commitment even before her death and before I read her journals. She was very matter-of-fact about her faith and the demands it placed on her life. That was just who she was. She talked to people about God when she worked at Subway. She reached out to strangers she met who needed help.

Nobody who ever knew her would doubt her commitment, and that is the main reason people accepted Richard Castaldo's account of her final moments. If you knew Rachel, her dying that way would make sense because that is the way she lived every moment of her life.

At the same time, I don't think she was some kind of religious fanatic. She was too real and too balanced to go to an extreme.

One of Rachel's journal entries was a song she had written

to encourage other people in their faith, but she felt the words convicting her to "walk her talk." She was too sensitive to browbeat others because she realized she wasn't perfect. She had sin and failure in her own life.

Father, reach out Your hand,
Grab a hold of my life.
Open my eyes,
To Your Wonderful light.
Fill me up,
With Your undying love.
Save me a place,
In Your kingdom above.

~by Rachel Joy Scott

I wrote this song, and when I wrote it, it was intended to motivate Christians to go preach the Gospel to the world. But by the time I got to the second verse, I realized that I should be talking to myself instead of everyone else. I should be taking my own advice. And as Christians, we need to remember to walk our talk.

Oalways!!!

Darrell and I had never been what you might call adamant fundamentalists, and Rachel wasn't either. We focused more on a daily walk, and we saw faith as a part of who we are. That's the way Rachel lived out her faith too.

We really tried to instill in our children the belief that it's not what you do externally so much as who you are internally that counts. And out of being who you are and your naturally flowing relationship with the Lord come all of the behaviors, the works of the Spirit. Rachel knew that living the life depended on being open to the leading of God's Spirit.

Darrell

Persecution or Pompous Christians?

Some Christians see conspiracies against believers everywhere. I personally think that in some cases, we have brought hostility on ourselves. Too often what we see on television or hear on the radio is a misrepresentation of true Christianity. As in any corporation, club, or organization, there are good people and there are bad. Unfortunately many have judged Christians by seeing a bad example.

It is true that there is a spiritual battle going on. It is true that there is a spirit in this world that is hostile to Christianity. But the weapons of our war are love, compassion, forgiveness, and kindness. These are hard to resist, even by the hardest heart. Rachel challenged us to start a chain reaction through acts of kindness. I encourage you, dear reader, to stop being "religious" and reach out to those around you in love and watch the amazing grace of God perform miracles.

I was appalled at the hatred and venom toward Christianity that I saw coming from the two boys who executed this tragic crime. As I watched their video diary, I was amazed at how many times they blasted the Christian faith. It appears that they had opened themselves up to spiritual influences that went beyond their control.

I believe that we live in a time in which the contrast

between light and darkness, good and evil, is becoming more apparent. There may be difficult days for Christians, but if we can "see through" our circumstances to "Him who is invisible," we cannot lose.

7 Creative Compassion

When Columbine senior Andrew Robinson finished writing *Smoke in the Room*, a play that would be performed by Columbine's aspiring actors and actresses in early April 1999, he knew he had a part custom-made for Rachel Scott, an expressive young woman who constantly explored numerous creative outlets.

Performing in the play required commitment from Rachel. Drama rehearsals were held on Monday and Wednesday nights, the same evenings that Rachel usually attended meetings of Breakthrough, a Christian youth ministry that challenged her to grow spiritually and surrounded her with supportive friends and elders.

Playing the part of Valerie also demanded a radical change in Rachel's appearance, something she embraced with open arms. Her family may have been surprised to see her cut off her beautiful brunette hair and dye what was left purple. But for Rachel, it was all part of what it took to convincingly portray a character who looked as if she was a part of the grunge-style alternative-rock subculture.

Throughout the months of rehearsal and preparation for the performance, Rachel wrote in her journal about how she missed her regular meetings with her Christian friends at Breakthrough. They missed her, too, though they supported her passion for acting, which was just one of many creative ways Rachel sought to reach out and build bridges to Columbine students.

"I loved how Rachel was at school," says Lori Johnson, Rachel's youth pastor with the Breakthrough group. "At Columbine, she didn't preach to people; she just was Jesus to people. She defied what a lot of churches say is the right way to evangelize people."

Audiences enjoyed *Smoke in the Room*, which was performed April 2–3, less than three weeks before the Columbine killings.

In many ways, the young girl who didn't know whether she wanted to be an actress or a missionary was actually both, continually finding creative ways to show people the compassion of Christ.

Beth

Being Real

I think that if there was one word to describe Rachel and the way she lived out her faith, it would be the word *real*. She had a deep sense of purpose in the way she communicated to people. I believe she made every effort to stay grounded in her relationship with the Lord so that her witness, in whatever form it was portrayed, would be perceived as being sincere and not superficial.

The interesting aspect of Rachel's witness is that she was able to express it in such enjoyable and refreshing ways. I loved to watch her perform and took great pleasure in seeing her in the high school play. Rachel had that touch, spark; call it many things, but she captured your heart.

The interests that Rachel pursued did not always come easily to her, and she did not take them lightly. Her pursuit of excellence often required her to work extremely hard to develop the skills she wanted. Rachel was studying forensics at school to improve her extemporaneous speaking. She traveled with the team to tournaments, which required much time and practice. Rachel was her own worst critic. She always saw the need for improvement and change. When she came home with a ribbon, I could sense her feeling of accomplishment. I was always proud of her, whether she placed or not. I was proud of her for trying and doing her best.

Rachel's recent project was to write a play for next year's spring performance. She already had worked out her outline and knew what the plot would be. Can you guess? Yes, it was going to be about a young person who did not fit in very well either with the family or at school (one of Rachel's beloved misfits). She had confidence that it was a topic she could explore and write about since it was an area she already had great passion for.

She loved music and usually had something playing all the time. She also enjoyed playing the piano, and for the most part she taught herself. The most recent piece of music she had learned was "My Heart Will Go On" from the *Titanic* sound track. Because of her love for this song, it was played at her memorial service and has become a symbol of how her family feels about her life.

Rachel had a very dramatic personality, and that was part of why drama and acting were so attractive to her. She loved her drama class, describing her elation in a passage from her journal.

Journal 1   1/7

Believable , Disclaimer , Passion

Ispirational. I feel like I can be stupid and I won't lose anything. I feel that I am passionate. I have a passion for life, God, and acting. I feel secure in this class. I feel like that the only way I can succeed is if express myself and get into things with a passion. I feel like I am with people that do not care what I do, as long as it's how I feel. Nothing here can scare me away. I feel comfortable. It's like this class brings out everything I love about theater. I like the activities coming up. I love the enthusiasm each person has for this class. I love how you have to be risky to go far. I love how it is not acceptable by the teacher and students if someone is mocking someone else. I love how much I am going to learn and how much my theater skills will improve. I love this class because it is inspirational

---

The joy that Rachel felt when she heard she had been chosen for the female lead in the play *Smoke in the Room* was unbelievable. She danced around the room and sparkled with unbridled happiness. Of course, we were happy with her. For her, it was the first step to reaching her goal of being onstage. Little did we know that it would be her only step.

Her character was a girl named Valerie who was judged negatively by people who looked only at her outward appearance. But inside, she was an extremely loving, giving, kind person. Hey—all Rachel had to do was get up onstage and be herself! She could not have been more elated by this part. What more could she ask for? She would be acting out everything she believed and was trying to live, right in front of her classmates.

I was surprised, no *shocked*, when Rachel got her hair cut for the part of Valerie. Couldn't she have just worn a wig? Well, I think so, but for Rachel that would not have been authentic. Why buy a wig when you have all of this beautiful brown hair that you are so willing to sacrifice for the sake of the cause? As the mom, I would have willingly paid for the wig, but Rachel's argument was, "It's got to be real, *Mom!*" Oh, well. It was just one more aspect of Rachel being so dramatic.

Rachel also threw herself into gathering props for the play. That explains the sudden disappearance of our spare refrigerator. One day as I was pulling into our garage, I noticed the refrigerator we kept out there was missing. I called Larry and asked him if he had any idea where it was. He was just as much in the dark as I was. Well, when Miss Rachel came home from working at Subway that evening, she conveniently informed us: "Mom, we need it for the school play. I had a couple of the guys come and pick it up." It never occurred to her that it might not be acceptable for her to arrange for someone to get it without clearing it with us first. Rachel had this little sweetness about her that worked for her *if* she needed to do any convincing for you to see things her way. For the next two weeks, our refrigerator was center stage in the school auditorium. She also took a blinking stoplight, a set of old car license plates, a purple lava lamp, and any other items from her bedroom that she felt would give the set a real college-room look. Rachel was certainly one to be as authentic as possible, and her impromptu personality came to life in such situations.

She enjoyed music, drama, art, and most expressions of creativity. For her, much of this was more than just entertainment or a hobby to pass time. It carried a much deeper level of personal expression and fulfillment that was completely hers and not a carbon copy of another work or an imitation of what someone else had already created.

In one of Rachel's journal entries, she contrasted human creations such as buildings and civilization with the beauty of nature. I believe this was her way of showing her appreciation for God's role as Creator.

> The earth's beauty has been reformed
> by the bricks man has laid
> She has taken years to give us
> these incredible scenes
> And we have destroyed it
> in a matter of months.
> I can no longer look at the
> purple glazed mountains
> I must first move my eyes
> past the constructions of man
> Man who has become obsessed
> with material possessions
> Man who has forgotten
> the beautiful earth that gives them life

When I think about words that express the way Rachel was, I think of words like *nontraditional, unorthodox,* and *contemporary*. She so desperately wanted her witness and faith to connect with simple effectiveness in this generation that being contemporary was of vital importance to her. Rachel was one to study and read the Word of God, and she was one to pray, but probably neither approach would be her first choice to introduce someone to a personal relationship with the Lord.

In her desire to be more approachable to her peers, she dressed in a nonconformist manner. She also went to parties and hung out with kids who were much different from her. As a mother, I had my concerns about all of this, and it would have been my tendency not to allow it, but I did. In all honesty, I was not always aware of everything she did.

There are places in the New Testament where Jesus went out and visited sinners, drunkards, and prostitutes—basically all the kinds of people who wouldn't be welcome in many religious circles today. Rachel had a heart for these people, and that took her to places where more "traditional" Christians wouldn't go.

Greetings from the Team

A few weeks after Rachel's funeral, I received a memory book from Rachel's friends who had been on the school drama with her. As I and the other family members read through the book, we found deep and meaningful writings that expressed how much the students had loved Rachel. But mixed in with all of the tributes was some language that we didn't understand or found shocking.

Two teachers involved in the drama program explained the

language to us in a cover letter that accompanied the memory book:

May 17, 1999
To Rachel's family:

As we read over the things that the team wrote to Rachel in the memory book, we realized that there is an inside joke you might need to have explained. In the last few years, the kids have taken to giving one another nick-names that are, in fact, the complete opposite of the people to whom they are given. You may notice that several of the kids refer to Rachel as "D.D.W." or "Dirty, Dirty Whore." At first glance, I would imagine that would be very shocking. They gave her this name because they admired Rachel's solid moral stand. In fact, she made it easier for team members to voice their own, high moral beliefs. It was always intended to emphasize the qualities that her team mates most respected in her, and we hope that you will understand this intention.

We cannot tell you enough how fortunate we feel to have had Rachel as a part of this team. All of our lives have been made better by her presence, as I am sure you will see in the heartfelt praise of her peers. Thank you so much for sharing your beautiful daughter with us.

I will be the first to admit that I initially found the language in some of the notes quite shocking. And as we would learn much later, Dylan Klebold had referred to Rachel as a "godly whore" in one of the horrible videotapes he and Eric Harris had created in the months before the shooting.

No mother wants to have her beautiful daughter called dirty names. But after reading the letter, although I still did not like their choice of words, I understood that the drama students were expressing their respect for Rachel in a contemporary, dramatic way. She must have taken it in stride and with good humor.

Often, church people seem to put all kinds of barriers in people's way before we will reach out to them. Sometimes we expect unchurched people to behave nicely, use pleasant language, and live sinless lives. But Jesus never put those kinds of barriers in people's way. He reached out to them, no matter where they were.

Rachel was able to connect with the members of the drama team, and it seems that God enabled her to touch them all very deeply. Amid uncertainty and her personal questioning at times, she felt God was using her.

Actress or Missionary?

I grew up in a traditional environment in which full-time ministry usually involved being a pastor or missionary or possibly singing Christian music. Darrell and I fell right in line with those ideals and followed in the footprints of our parents. At some point, what was considered to be orthodox ministry took on a different aspect for us, and we began to see the church outside the church walls. I believe our change helped Rachel to have the confidence and courage to step outside the traditional boundaries and embrace a Christian lifestyle that did not limit God. We were pleased and proud of Rachel's exuberance to explore her faith in a real world with real people.

During the last couple of years of her life, I think Rachel

was torn about what she wanted to do. One journal entry describes her feelings.

> Dear God,
>
> Why do I feel dry in Your Spirit? Why do I feel that the fire has died within me, yet so many claim they see the light of You, oh God, burning brightly? Why do I have to feel moments of doubt, distrust, disbelief, stages of anger, & stages of loneliness when it comes to you, Father? Why do I lose focus of You during praise & worship as well as prayer? Why can't I completely be consumed by You? Why can't I be used by You? Why do I feel self-righteous at times? Why do I feel afraid?

Rachel's dreams of becoming an actress probably had less to do with being onstage or in films than with having an outlet for contemporary expression and creative ministry.

She had been planning on going on a Teen Mania missions trip to Africa during the summer of 1999. She had written her support letter more than a year before and was anxiously awaiting her opportunity.

As the Lord would have it, Rachel never got to make that trip, but Larry and I were privileged to go for her. We were invited by the Life Outreach International Ministry of James Robison in early August 1999 to travel to Angola for a special "feed the children" outreach. In South Africa, we teamed up with the Jesus Alive Ministries, which establish many feeding programs throughout much of Africa.

Upon leaving Johannesburg, we flew in the *Life Angel* aircraft that is a carrier of food and supplies to the innermost parts of Africa. The plane was completely packed from top to bottom with everything from our personal drinking water to the basic soup ingredients to be given to the thousands of starving children.

Our first stop after our arrival in Angola was a children's graveyard. That was the most painful experience we had in Africa because that day was August 5, Rachel's eighteenth birthday. Larry and I walked by row after row of little graves, many just three-feet-long mounds of dirt. Most of the graves had no markers except for a little blanket, maybe a little home-made cross, or possibly a dried flower or two.

While we stood there and wept and wept, I was overcome with the knowing of a mother's heart at burying a child who had died because of the violence of malnutrition and disease. My thoughts went to Rachel and how her heart would have been broken to see the suffering of so many because of having so little. During that week, we went to many villages and feeding stations to minister the very basics of Christian love.

Just as Rachel would have given the shirt off her back to help meet the need, Larry and I knew we would always carry Rachel's burden to minister to Africa and other missions outreaches.

No Experience Required

In too many instances we complicate simple acts of love and kindness by trying to cloak them in a religious form. One young lady named Jessica, who sent an E-mail to us, relayed this incident: "I met Rachel at a gas station. I was short five cents so she pulled a nickel out of her pocket and set it on the counter. When I asked her who she was, she told me this: 'Rachel Scott, good to meet you, friend.' I didn't know her, but her kindness and her smile has stuck with me even though it is three years later."

Simple love and kindness will make a lasting impression on a person's heart as they did with a young man I will call Jim (not his real name). Jim was a student at Columbine High School who suffered with a number of physical disabilities. The young man was basically left to fend for himself and was not surrounded by friends. His life had been lonely and one struggle after another with few happy days. Rachel took notice of this young man and, with a compassionate heart, crossed the invisible line that keeps so many of us from reaching out. She befriended Jim and made an effort to give him acceptance and the desperately needed love of a friend.

Rachel asked Jim if he had ever had a date. He was embarrassed and said, "No." "Well," said Rachel, "then I am asking you for a date." Jim was thrilled! Not only did he have a date, but she was pretty too. He was looking forward to going to a movie and supper. The events of April 20 cut short Jim's dreams of going out with Rachel. She would never be able to keep that date. In the days that followed, Jim's mother told us how he cried and said, "Now I have no friends at school anymore." The one cherished moment in the life of a very lonely young man is that one person dared to reach out, expecting nothing in return, and gave simple love and kindness.

Significance comes with knowing who you are, not with what you do. Rachel was learning that and making every effort to put it into practice. I remember a reporter asking me once, "Do you think Rachel was a part of cliques or groups like that?" "No," I told her. "I doubt she was, but if she had wanted to be a part of a clique, she probably would form her own. She would have brought all the misfits and kids that fall through the cracks at school together and made them feel accepted and special."

Rachel did reach out, even to the killers. She shared a photo-video class with them. When the boys turned in their violent video that depicted their fantasies of death and destruction, Rachel turned in a photo assignment of the hand picture that is illustrated in this book. Months before April 20, there was a spiritual battle waging between good and evil in the halls of Columbine. The teachers did not challenge the boys' project, the administration did not check it out, and their parents were not aware of what they had produced. But Rachel knew. Rachel stepped out on a limb and challenged Eric and Dylan about why they were so obsessed with killing and death. She tried to find out why they would produce something of that nature. She wanted to help them and possibly paid with her life for daring to do what no one else was willing to do.

8 No Solitary Soul

The spring of 1999 had been one of the most hectic periods in Rachel Scott's busy life. In addition to attending classes at Columbine High School, she had an active social life, and she worked part-time at a Subway sandwich shop. The highlight of her week was her youth group.

Breakthrough was the youth ministry group at Orchard Road Christian Center, the Assemblies of God congregation located off I-25. It was Rachel's sister Dana who brought her into contact with Breakthrough, which would change the rest of her life. Here is how Dana remembers that process:

How does one begin? For someone like me, it seems so impossible to write some of the most important things to me about Rachel or to make someone really understand and see

115

how priceless my memories are with her. It's strange how important and how sacred every memory and every picture has become. When I see her picture, I often just stare and wonder what it would be like to enter that picture and remember what it was like when Rachel was still here. Rachel was always so much better at expressing her feelings in writing. She has really inspired me to write more things down. Even if they don't make sense, it helps to just write.

I feel like out of everyone in my family, God has given me a unique and special memory with Rachel that I wouldn't trade for anything in the world. I got to see something that no one else in my family had the privilege to see.

The last two years or so of Rachel's life, she and I went to the same youth group called Breakthrough. I remember the first time I invited her to come. I had started my involvement a few months earlier when a good friend of mine invited me to come, and I knew from the start that this place was exactly what my heart had been looking for. My life and love for God were being renewed, and this was just the beginning for me. I was so excited when Rachel decided to give it a chance. I couldn't wait for her to see how *on fire* and *alive* it was! We sat in the back together, and the whole time, during praise and worship, during prayer, during the lesson, I just kept giving her this look of, *See I told you you'd love it*. The problem was, though, that she didn't look that terribly impressed (probably because I was annoying the snot out of her by staring the whole time). When I asked her how she liked it afterward, she said, "Oh . . . it was okay." I was like, "What? How could you *not* think that this is the most awesome youth group ever?" Apparently, she didn't really like it at first, but that didn't last long. God ended up plugging her in there anyway.

It wasn't long after that when I began to see dramatic changes take place in Rachel's life. Her priorities and passions were changing, and she was spending so much more time in prayer and Bible reading that I was a little weirded out at first. She got real intense and passionate about making sure that we never missed a Breakthrough service. She became a leader in her cell group (even before I did), and I watched as she began to disciple and pour into people's lives, particularly over the phone. She spent countless hours on the phone for every occasion (and at graveyard hours in the night, no less). She had a way of teaching people that I didn't recognize as a gift she had until now. People listened and understood Rachel because she was very *real* with people about her Christianity. She was *real* about her relationship with God, and it impacted people in tremendous ways because they knew she was speaking from her heart. She communicated her concerns, her questions, and her triumphs of serving a living God. She didn't hand people watered-down, shmoopy-poopy, Bible-thumping verbal religious garbage that no one gets. She spoke in a language of honesty that anyone could interpret as *real*. People want truth, and she lived and spoke truth in the purest way possible, not by trying to follow Jesus' example, not by being an imitator, but by allowing Jesus to live the life He gives freely inside her! There is a huge difference!

There was one time of the week that belonged to just Rachel and me. Every Wednesday night I would come home from work and pick Rachel up to go to Breakthrough. We had a twenty-minute commute together, and it seemed like the only time lately when we really talked. We talked about how she was doing at school, how work was going for me, who she had her eye on at the time, and we even prayed together at times. We also loved to listen to "Five Iron Frenzy" songs and sing obnoxiously loud to them. Although twenty minutes may not seem like a long time, it couldn't have been spent more perfectly. We drove along having fun and hanging out as best friends, just like sisters ought to. We were five years apart in age and worlds apart as far as differences go, but those few moments spent together in the car God had completely reserved for just us, sisters.

During Breakthrough, I had the opportunity to see Rachel grow in the Lord that no one else in my family had the chance to see. I got to see her sing her lungs out and praise God with all her heart. I got to see her dance before the Lord and worship Him any way she wanted to. I got to see her fight her battles on her knees in prayer and really cry out to God during her times of need. I got to see her go and lay hands on friends' shoulders and pray over them and with them. She cried with them, focusing on the love for them and their needs instead of her own. When we were at Breakthrough together, I got to see her standing, kneeling, and lying down in God's presence, always wanting more. I got to see where she got her strength, her joy, her dreams, her inspiration, her wisdom, her boldness, her humility, her honesty, her passion to see lives touched by God, her anointing, her gifts, her talents, her gentleness, her creativity, her discernment, her acceptance of her position in God, her acceptance of herself, her acceptance of others, her ability to see the "brighter" side, her ability to see the "bigger picture," her compassion, her understanding, her quest for knowledge, her quest for truth, her open mind, her open heart, her selflessness, her peace of mind, her awesome sense of humor, her freedom from sin, her faith like a child, her hope, her love for people, and her love for God! I got to see

God mold my sister into something beautiful because her heart was willing to allow Him to do so. That beauty radiated outwardly, but more importantly, it came from within, and she didn't even know.

I believe with all my heart that God knew exactly what He was doing when He put Rachel in my mother's womb. I believe with all my heart that every desire that Rachel honestly had has been fulfilled. I know that no matter what the last thing I said about Rachel was, good or not so good, that no matter what my last thoughts of her were while she was still alive, there are no last words. Even if I could have another earthly moment with her, no words or actions would be good enough. There is no match to what I feel and know to be true in my heart about Rachel. God chose to take Rachel and set her by His side eternally, and I know that His ways are not our ways, and I trust the plan that He is carrying out with all my heart. After all, He didn't have to give me Rachel for seventeen years in the first place. But He did, and I love Him even more for that.

The group was Rachel's spiritual lifeline. She was a leader of one of the ministry's small groups, which met on Monday evenings, and she participated in the ministry's larger youth worship services on Wednesday evenings.

During the months that she was rehearsing for the play, Rachel deeply missed her time with her supportive peers at Breakthrough and the leaders who had meant so much to the growth and development of her spiritual life. She regularly wrote about her feeling of absence from the group.

After performing the play in early April, Rachel returned to Breakthrough, where members of the group and its youth minister, Lori Johnson, welcomed her back with open arms.

But the group's reunion with Rachel would be short-lived. Not long after she returned to the regular meetings of Breakthrough, Rachel was gunned down at Columbine. Her death deeply upset Lori, a Columbine graduate, along with the group's many loyal members, who had supported Rachel's dramatic aspirations and prolonged absence from the group, but longed to have her back in their midst once again.

Here, Lori tells about how she thinks back to the last times she saw Rachel.

Lori

Lingering Regrets

I saw Rachel in the play they did at Columbine. I had just gotten home that day from a nine-day missions trip with the group to Mexico. We passed out tracts, handed out Bibles, did presentations in churches, and talked to hundreds of people about getting saved.

Rachel couldn't go because of the play, but her sister Dana went on the trip, and she enjoyed working with churches in the jungles of northeastern Mexico.

We tried to do two missions trips every year, one during spring break time and another during the summer. The summer after Rachel's death we went to South Korea. I don't know if Rachel would have been on that trip because she was trying to raise money to go to Africa with Teen Mania. She was looking forward to that so much.

Rachel came to our Breakthrough meeting the first Wednesday night after the play because she didn't have practices anymore. I can still remember seeing her smiling face as she came bounding up to me.

"Hey, I want to talk to you," she said.

"I want to talk to you too," I said.

It was a busy week, and I didn't see Rachel at church over the weekend. She often had to work on Sundays. Some weekends she participated in forensic competitions. And other times she attended church elsewhere, with either her mom or her dad.

The following Monday night, God put it on my heart to call Rachel. I had a feeling that I really needed to talk to her. But I didn't call. And the next day she was killed.

I think that's probably my greatest personal regret about all of this. We had been very close. At Breakthrough, we had a number of small groups of twenty to thirty kids that met on Monday nights, and Rachel was a student leader in the group I was in charge of. I often went by her house to pick her up and take her to the meetings. We had wonderful talks.

But that Monday, I would have really liked to have had a chance to have another conversation with her. I would have loved to know what she was thinking about and what was going on with her that night.

Beth

Streams of Living Water

Like many large high schools, Columbine had an established Christian prayer group. The Columbine group organized weekly meetings at the school and participated in big annual events like See You at the Pole.

Some of the Christians killed at Columbine were connected to this group, but Rachel was not a big part of it. She knew the kids who were in the group, and some of them have told me that they knew Rachel. They knew she was a Christian, and they knew what she stood for.

But if you knew Rachel, you would understand that she wouldn't have been comfortable being a member of a school prayer club. For her, I think that was a little bit too much of a traditional Christian thing to do. And sometimes these groups become in-groups at school, and Rachel didn't want to be a part of any in-group. She wanted to relate to anybody and everybody. She supported the prayer club, but that was not where her heartbeat was. However, as we learned later, this prayer club played an invaluable part in what took place on April 20, 1999. As the club met throughout the year, a theme was birthed and became a prophetic prayer. That simple prayer was, "God, use our school to touch the world." Little did anyone know how literally that prayer would be answered.

Breakthrough was Rachel's primary source of spiritual strength and solace, as she indicated in her journals. She drew her life from Breakthrough, she drew her inspiration from there, and that's where she found much of her encouragement and her motivation to be a committed Christian. That's where she fed herself, that's where she got her strength to be able to be the kind of Christian she tried to be at school, and that's where she was very plugged in.

Except for the months before her death, when she was so involved in rehearsals for the school play, she went to Breakthrough meetings at least twice a week. On Monday nights small groups met at various homes, and on Wednesday nights they had their whole youth group and worship service.

Dear Heavenly Father,

You are too good God. Thank you for the people at Breakthru. They truly help me keep my focus on you. Please keep watch over Jeff and Luke. I am so happy now that I have been to walk my talk. Remember when I asked for heads to turn in the halls when I passed by? I think a few people took a second look. Thanks for the light you have put in me. That light has had conviction on my friends. I don't have to say anything... they just see you in me.

Rachel Joy

And a lot of times they would do other activities, such as missions trips or ski trips.

Giving and Taking

Rachel was a leader, so she gave to the group, but she received from the other kids in the group too. During the Monday night small group meetings at a member's house, Rachel had a lot of personal needs met by the kids in her group.

If she was struggling with something, that's where her peers ministered to her. They did Bible studies together, they prayed together, and they shared openly about the challenges and struggles they were going through.

She often described what the group meant to her in her journals. The following entry was written less than a month before her death.

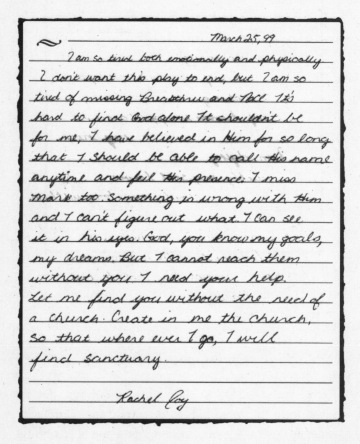

> March 25, 99
>
> I am so tired both emotionally and physically. I don't want this play to end, but I am so tired of missing Breakthru and all. It's hard to find God alone. It shouldn't be for me. I have believed in Him for so long that I should be able to call His name anytime and feel His presence. I miss Mark too. Something is wrong with Him and I can't figure out what. I can see it in his eyes. God, you know my goals, my dreams. But I cannot reach them without you. I need your help. Let me find you without the need of a church. Create in me the church, so that where ever I go, I will find sanctuary.
>
> Rachel Joy

I know from talking to Rachel and her sister Dana that Breakthrough is a praying group. Prayer isn't something they talk about but never do; they devote a lot of time and energy to praying.

Often when Rachel went to the Breakthrough meetings, she came back so late at night that I wouldn't see her until the next morning. It was not unusual to hear her coming in at midnight or one in the morning, long after we had already turned in.

Of course, some of what she was doing was fun. Not all of it was serious time with the Lord. But I trusted Rachel thoroughly, and I knew that Breakthrough was a safe environment. At other places, you're not sure your kids are always safe, but I didn't worry about Breakthrough meetings. The group has good leaders who have been trustworthy, responsible, and mature. I have always trusted them to keep things in check.

Early in the evening, before Rachel went to Breakthrough, all she could think of was getting ready and getting out the door. A lot of times she wouldn't eat supper. Eating was less important to her than being with the people she loved and trusted. She was adamant about not missing the meetings, even in bad weather and even when she had to work at Subway. On work days, she went from school to Subway, and from Subway to Breakthrough. On days when she didn't have to work, she enjoyed riding to the meetings with Lori. Lori and Rachel connected on a deep level.

Lori

No Solo Christian

Rachel loved the fellowship and acceptance she had with her friends at Breakthrough. It was a safe environment where there was nothing that had to be proved. Acceptance by peers and leaders made it a comfortable place to be. A person could be at any point of spiritual growth and not experience embarrassment, but only be encouraged to take the next step to a higher level. At Breakthrough, Rachel saw mentors and leaders who inspired her to be faithful, but not overwhelmed by the challenge of growing. The youth group also gave kids a real handle on how to face their issues and imparted a love for the Word of God that would prove to have all the answers. The teaching from leaders gave confidence to the kids that was encouraging and promoted in them the desire to pursue God.

One of the handouts we used in a Breakthrough study revealed the source of Rachel's confidence. In the margin of the sheet we used a year before her death, she talked about "Christ-esteem."

A Burning Light

Rachel was a unique person, and there were so many things that attracted me to her. She loved drama, and she was a dramatic person, even when she wasn't performing. I also liked the way she dressed, which was really original. It was as if she would play different parts. One day she would dress in a preppy style, and another day she would dress in an alternative look.

In so many ways, Rachel was really artistic, but she never did the "moody artist" routine. She was a happy person who made people around her laugh a lot. But she was also a deep person. She felt deeply about many things. And she was confident.

But if I had to say one thing that represented Rachel for me,

✱ Romans 5 (Britt)
✱ Galations 2:20

Pastor Todd Walker   Breakthrough   April 25, 1998

Desperate Measures

I. We live in a desperate world.

Since October, their have been 4 school-related shooting, killing 10 and injuring 22.

WHY?

A. The world is desperate to end the loneliness and pain

B The world is desperate to be at peace with itself

C. The world is desperate for answers.

II. We are a worldly church **if we are desperate for what the world is desperate.**

self-esteem is irrelivant Christ-esteem is what is important we may not think that we are not good enough but Jesus loved us enough that he died for us, and thought we were good enough for that sacrifice, we are not worthy... but he loved us enough to do it anyway

Romans 12:2 "Do not conform any longer to the pattern of this world, but be transformed by the renewing of your mind..."

A. Where is the faith spoken of in the Bible?

1. Faith brings peace.
   Romans 5:1

2. Faith brings joy.
   Romans 5:2

3. Faith says, "I don't need answers, I need God. I don't need to have every thing go the way I want, I need God to continue His work in me."
   Romans 5:3-5

B. It's hard to be desperate, when you are dead.

Gal 2:20 "I have been crucified with Christ and I no longer live, but Christ lives in me. The life I live in the body, I live by faith in the Son of God, who loved me and gave himself for me." (christ lives in me)

1

I would have to say that it was her passion. She had a lot of passion about things. I think the strongest was her passion for God. She was very passionate about knowing God and serving God. She was also passionate about her family. She was always trying to get family members to come to Breakthrough. They would always come up with excuses, but she wouldn't let that stop her. And she was passionate for her friends. She cared very deeply about all kinds of people at Columbine.

Rachel once told me that at school she had sat at a lunch table one day with a group of kids. She looked around, and everybody else was black or Hispanic. She was the only white person at the table, and she loved that.

It was interesting to me that Rachel never had a particular clique that she always hung out with. Instead, she looked out for people who seemed to need a friend and befriended them. She didn't care what someone looked like or whether or not he was "cool." She was fascinated with people, and I mean *all* people.

Not the Center of Attention

Rachel was attractive and confident, but in a big youth ministry of two hundred people like ours, she never really stuck out. People coming to the group for the first time might not have noticed her because she was not up front a lot, other than in some of the dramas she did at our retreat.

But in our small group, which had about thirty kids, she really did shine because her passion for God was so very strong. She wanted to do something for God with her life, and for her, a big part of that involved the kids she knew at Columbine.

Rachel was a leader in our small group. She was part of a student leadership team that ran the group, planned activities, and organized our programs. She wrote some of the discussion sheets that we use every week in smaller groups of five or six kids to talk about various issues and problems people are going through. She also made it a habit to greet every visitor she could see, and she followed up with some of the kids who had come to the group, giving them a call and getting involved in their lives.

She gave a lot to the group, but I think Rachel got a lot out of the group. There were adults like me who discipled her, which helped her to be motivated to know God even more. Rachel told me that it really helped her to have such a strong base of friends who were strong in God too.

Deep Calling unto Deep

Rachel loved being alone with God, and there were times she believed she heard from God very clearly. One Sunday morning she came into one of our leadership meetings and, with her face shining brightly, said, "Lori, I heard from God today."

I remember her telling me about it:

I woke up today really early, and after I woke up, I felt like I should take a walk. So I went to take a walk with God.

I went to the park while it was still dark, and saw the sun rise through the trees. Then God spoke to me and said, *You can see the sun. Yes, you can see it in part. But you can only see the sun shining from behind the trees. You don't really see the sun clearly yet.*

Soon, the sun rose higher up in the morning sky, above the trees, and I heard God saying to me, *That's the same way it is with Me. You used to hear Me in part. You used to have a picture of Me in part. But now you're going to see Me more clearly.*

Rachel told me about that experience sometime in early

1998. For the rest of her life, that experience was a foundational one for her, and her life seemed to take on a deeper spiritual dimension.

Much of the time, the things Rachel heard from God inspired her and encouraged her. But some of these things made her sorrowful, and some even gave her a sense of foreboding about the future.

During 1998, I used to go by Rachel's house and pick her up for Breakthrough's small group meeting. On some of these rides, she talked to me about the sense of foreboding she seemed to be getting from God or somewhere. She had a growing premonition that she was dying or would not be alive for very long. She told me she thought something was "wrong" inside, but she didn't know what it was.

One of her journal entries describes some of these feelings.

Eternity Now

Breakthrough Retreat   3-7-98
God... I have this terrible sharp, dull pain in my stomach. I don't know if it's a spiritual feeling, if the enemy is attacking, or if its just sickness whatever it is, I just ask for your healing. If it's a spiritual feeling, I ask you to bless it. If it's the enemy, I ask you to bind it. If it's just sickness I ask you to heal it. Thank you

Rachel Joy

Part of this time, she wasn't really eating, and she wasn't really sleeping. I kept telling her that she needed to have her mom take her to the doctor to have her blood tested. I thought she might have had a terminal disease or something. She went to the doctor, but the tests didn't find anything wrong. She believed that the pain might have been something God had given her to increase her sensitivity to the pain of the world.

There were times when Rachel had a little bit of sadness I could sense around her. At times I thought she was ill or maybe depressed, but at other times I thought that she really had a lot of insight that God had given her, and that she had seen something bad was going to happen.

April 20

Thinking back to the events of that day, I remember seeing Cassie Bernall's photo on a television newscast and thinking, *Why does that girl look really familiar to me?* It turns out she had visited Breakthrough. The group also knew Lauren Townsend, who died at Columbine. In a strange way, I knew three of the dead young people. But nobody who died was as close to our group as Rachel.

The first I heard about the Columbine shootings was about 11.30 that morning when I walked into one of our big meeting rooms at church, and a girl there said, "Hey, don't you know someone who goes to Columbine? You need to listen to the radio."

I didn't think anything of it. I didn't really understand the magnitude of what was happening at Columbine until somebody came in and said that people were dead.

Our church has a media department with all different kinds of TVs, so I was watching news on three channels simultaneously. Then it hit me. "Oh, my gosh," I said to myself, "Rachel's at this school." Beginning at that moment, I had the experience that time was standing still. It was very surreal.

While I was watching the tragedy unfold on TV, I got a call from Samantha, who was one of Rachel's really good friends. Everybody called her Sam. Sam, who goes to Cherry Creek High School, was crying over the phone. I took the rest of the day off and went over to be with her.

We called Rachel's house and were told that Craig had come home with blood all over his clothes. "Please call when Rachel comes home," we said. Day turned into nighttime, but we still hadn't heard anything about Rachel. People from Breakthrough were at Sam's watching TV, but nobody was eating. We couldn't. We were just sitting there waiting for the phone to ring. But it didn't ring.

Around ten o'clock that night, one of our pastors called me outside and said, "Lori, you have to realize at this point that she's probably dead." I hoped it wasn't true, but I gradually accepted it. I remember crying and being really sad.

Then I realized that someone was going to need to tell Sam, who was sixteen at the time. Everybody else left the house, but I stayed with Sam all night upstairs in her room. We cried a lot and talked about Rachel. I don't know exactly how long we sat and talked, but we must have been up until 1:30 or 2:00 the next morning, crying and talking and coming to terms with it.

About six o'clock that morning, Sam got up and started getting ready to go to school. Her parents had told her that she could stay home from school if she wanted, but Sam wanted to go. She told me: "You know, I have prayed for so long for an opportunity to make an impact for Christ at Cherry Creek. I know that if I go to school today, people who know I was Rachel's friend will ask me how I am doing, and I can tell them that I am okay because of Jesus."

Aftermath

That was Wednesday morning. Long before this, Breakthrough had scheduled a special outreach service for that evening. I was overwhelmed and didn't know what to do. What do you say at a time like that? I was kind of mad at God, to be honest. "I can't believe You are making me do this when I just lost my friend," I said.

I was in shock, and I could feel the adrenaline rushing through my body. Then God spoke to me and said, *Lori, you've always wanted to do something that would impact this city for Me. Don't resent the place that I've given you in this time. I've given you a voice to be able to talk to a bunch of people who are hurting. You've got a chance to tell them there is hope.* I cried and said, "You're right, God."

We went ahead with the outreach service, giving people a place to come and cry. We decided to give them a place to sit, talk about what had happened, and be sad or angry if they wanted to without us telling them that everything would suddenly be all better. We wanted to provide a safe place where people could express how they felt about the whole tragedy.

Usually we have 180 to 200 kids on a Wednesday night. That night about 400 people came. At some time during the evening, we lit a candle and had a moment of silence for the young people and the teacher who had died the previous day.

Rachel's funeral was on Saturday. After the service, the casket was opened. I was still struggling with understanding the whole thing, but when I saw her, it really hit me. She's dead. I was able to say good-bye to her then.

The next Monday we had our small group meeting—the meeting that Rachel would have attended had she been alive. At that meeting I spoke very openly about some of the things I had realized in the aftermath of the tragedy.

The End of a Dream

At our meeting I talked about my feeling of shock. I felt so strange that such a tragedy had happened at my old school in suburban Littleton, Colorado. Many people tend to think that their neighborhood with their homes and schools is safe, but the events at Columbine shattered that for me. Now I don't think there is a safe place in this world anymore.

I know that I have to reach beyond this world for true safety and security because I won't be getting what I need here. True security lies in heaven, where things can't be touched by evil and can't be destroyed.

For a long time I had known that the Bible taught about how our lives, this world, and everything in it are passing, but after Columbine I began to understand what the teaching meant.

My new understanding totally changed the way I approach youth ministry. I no longer look at high school students as carefree people who are living their fun-filled years.

More than ever before, I understand that we're in a spiritual war between good and evil. I see that each day at school could have very serious implications for students. And I now know that any day, the students' lives could be taken from them.

A Crown of Life

I think often of Rachel. She had such awesome dreams, and all of her dreams included God.

Rachel and Sam used to talk about how they wanted to live as the apostle Paul did—on the edge with total dependence on God.

I'm not angry at God anymore for allowing Rachel to be taken. She wanted to impact people for God. Through her death, she touched the world, and she still touches the world today. I believe that if she had known what was going to happen to her, she would do it all over again. Her life was cut short, but God saw to it that her dream for her life was fulfilled.

At her funeral, I could picture a coronation taking place in heaven. I thought, *Wow, at seventeen years of age, she is receiving a crown of life*.

Craig had just started going with Rachel to Breakthrough when she was killed. Attending cell group and youth group meetings has since become the most important part of his week. Breakthrough has helped him work through many of the painful, traumatic experiences he suffered in the library on April 20. Here is how he remembers Rachel:

> As I sit here in my sister's room writing with only the light from her scented candles (she loved candles), I remember Rachel. Rachel and I were normal brother and sister. We had our petty fights, said things we didn't mean, and shared our good times. I miss that so much. I wish I had her back, but she would not come back. That was her dream: to be used by God, to change lives. She wouldn't trade it back.

Rachel was just a normal girl willing to be used by God to start a chain reaction of love. I want to do the same thing. I want to continue her love chain that demonstrated itself by kindness and friendship and keep it going.

I remember riding in her red Acura on our way to school. She would be in the driver's seat, and I would be on the passenger's side. We'd be driving down streets with beautiful white trees, white sidewalks, white yards all covered with snow, listening to "Bittersweet Symphony" or "Jewel" or maybe favorite songs on the radio. We would park in Clement Park, which is next to Columbine High School. As we hopped out of the car with our backpacks, the melodies of the songs we had been listening to would be playing in our minds.

We had to walk along an icy trail to reach the front of the school. It would be freezing out! Our hands would be so cold, and we would rejoice when at last we would pass through the cold metal doors into the warmth of the school and be able to feel the heat. She would go one way down the hall, and I went the other way. "C-ya," we quickly said. I don't get to do that anymore.

A characteristic I remember about Rachel was that her love for people was less conditional than anyone I knew of her age or in the school. It didn't matter to her what you looked like or who your friends were. I loved that about her. Another thing I liked and respected so much was that she made it clear for herself and others what her beliefs were. I hope to be able to do the same.

I believe in God. He saved me from death that same day. He

took my sister's life from this earth, and I trust Him that He did the best thing. I want to be able to pick up where she had to let it go and continue her witness.

I love you, Rachel, and we *will* meet again.

Love, Craig

A POEM AND DRAWING ABOUT RACHEL BY HER BROTHER, MICHAEL SCOTT

RACHEL IS MY LITTLE LAMB WITH HURTING
EYES BECAUSE SHE SEES THIS EVIL WORLD
THAT IS BLINDING HER EYES WITH TEARS. SHE
WAS WILLING TO DIE TO MAKE A DIFFERENCE.
SHE IS CHANGING THE WORLD THROUGH HER
DIARIES AND HER FAMILY. HER TEARS AND
HER DEATH ARE NOT IN VAIN. GOD BLESS OUR
LITTLE LAMB. I LOVE YOU RACHEL.

YOUR BROTHER, MIKE SCOTT

9 Parenting with Grace and Love

BETHANEE, LARRY, MIKE, BETH, CRAIG, DANA, AND RACHEL

Perhaps one of the greatest challenges of parenting is trying to create a loving and safe environment in which children can do two things: (1) learn to make wise choices; and (2) enjoy life and all the adventures and still survive the struggles involved in growing into healthy adulthood.

Achieving the proper balance between the firm discipline needed for learning and the freedom needed for creativity and individuality isn't always easy. There are times when parents run the risk of becoming too rigid and legalistic.

Rachel's parents were raised in homes where more emphasis was placed on fearing God than on loving God. In trying to correct that approach with their children, they believe they created an environment that helped Rachel understand God's amazing grace.

Darrell

Parenting with Grace

There's a passage in Paul's letter to the Philippians in which the apostle appeared to brag about his outward legalism: "In regard to the law, a Pharisee . . . as for legalistic righteousness, faultless." Only two verses later, though, Paul confessed the error of his former ways, declaring that all his earlier self-righteous activities were so much garbage: "I consider them rubbish, that I may gain Christ and be found in him, not having a righteousness of my own that comes from the law, but that which is through faith in Christ—the righteousness that comes from God and is by faith" (Phil. 3:5–6, 8–9).

I really understand where Paul was coming from in these verses. I have tasted the fruit of legalism, and I can tell you that it does not produce life. I have also tasted the fruit of grace, and I can tell you that it is rich and sweet!

I appreciate my Christian upbringing, even if I disagree with some things about it. One of the major changes in my life took place when I began to realize that the very efforts put forth to become holy or righteous become the barriers that prevent it from happening.

I have tried to teach my children that Christianity is not a set of rules and regulations that make them good people. It is first and foremost a relationship with God through His Son, Jesus Christ. Then the key to a successful Christian walk is letting Jesus live His life through you.

When I was in high school, I had such a desire to be pleasing to God. I faithfully fasted every Thursday, and I attempted to pray one hour every day. However, I walked in frustration because no matter how much I worked at it, I never seemed to come to peace with myself as being a righteous or holy person. Years later I was to understand why. All of our self-righteousness is filthy rags to God. He's not interested in us performing for Him or trying to impress Him with a multitude of rules and regulations. That's exactly what Jesus warned His disciples about: the leaven of the Pharisees.

What He wants is honesty. He wants us to recognize our weaknesses and submit them to Him. This is the doorway to grace and fulfillment. He resists the proud and gives grace to the humble. Rachel had a tremendous impact on her classmates at school because she walked in grace. She allowed God to express Himself through her.

Parenting by Principle

In the process of raising our children, I never had a strict list of do's and don'ts. Instead, I talked to the kids about principles, and I encouraged them to be open and honest with me about how they applied these principles.

With this approach parents will be taking a risk with their children. Parenting by principle means spending more time talking to kids, explaining the purpose that principles are designed to produce, and discussing whether particular behaviors support or violate the principles. Principles are more subtle than rules, and kids are great at finding creative ways to interpret and avoid them.

Teaching my kids through principles rather than rules was an effective way to get at the deeper issues of obedience and character, issues that can all too often be totally ignored when families talk about only detailed rules and regulations. In controversial areas such as music and movies, for example, focusing on principle gets to the heart of the matter of what a particular song or film is about rather than relying on external criteria such as musical styles ("rock is bad, but country is good").

Parenting by principle helps us avoid becoming victims of a mysterious but powerful phenomenon that can be stated as follows: "The law simply magnifies the temptation." If you tell a child not to do a particular thing, the very telling seems to increase the interest in the act. If you slap an "R" rating on a film or a "Parental Advisory" sticker on a CD, some kids will feel an inescapable urge to want to know firsthand what led to the rating or the sticker.

Principles can help us avoid both the temptations and the legalism often associated with rules and regulations.

Raising a Mystic

Reading Rachel's journals, I am repeatedly struck by the depth of her intimacy with God and the strength of her desire to grow closer to God on a daily basis. I don't claim credit for her beautiful spiritual life, but I believe that Rachel's understanding of grace contributed to her desire to know God and love Him more deeply.

Rachel grew up understanding God primarily as Someone who loved and cared for her, and the rules God laid down for her life were seen as helpful guides to keep her from hurting herself. Rules were not the main issue. Loving God was priority number one, and the guidelines for living came through that.

I know that Rachel experimented with smoking, and I

know that she was tempted to drink. That would drive some parents crazy, but I don't think either behavior threatened Rachel's relationship with God or her eternal life. She was exploring her freedom and testing the waters.

A brief entry in one of Rachel's journals describes the tension between following God and following the wishes of religious people. I think the passage illustrates that she was trying to follow the will of God, not the dictates of man.

> Rafting trip   June 13, 98
> I struggle Father, I seek the blessing of holy people instead of the Holy One. Help me, oh God

Rachel's understanding of her freedom before God helped her love God more deeply, and I believe it gave her the freedom and security to be herself, to find meaningful ways to express her love for God, and to develop her creative ways of talking to other people about God. Her freedom before God helped her to be free with others, and the people who knew her were attracted to that kind of loving and liberating dedication to God.

Beth

A Mother-to-Be's Prayers

When I became pregnant with Bethanee, I started praying for wisdom from God. I didn't want to be like those people who say, "If only I knew then what I know now, I would have done things differently." I wanted to know *now,* and I asked God to give me wisdom right away.

I prayed for the entire nine months of my pregnancy, and when I wasn't praying, I became a student of parenting. I bought and read dozens of Christian parenting books, which were becoming more popular during the 1970s. Like a sponge soaks up water in a desert, I saturated myself with principles of parenting discussed in those books.

Even my Bible studies during that nine-month period were focused on relationships: how God related to us, how we should relate to each other, and how parents should relate to their children. I became consumed with learning how to be a loving and godly parent, and in the process, how I looked at things underwent an enormous evolution. I came away with a new understanding of children and how to deal with problems and discipline. Everything that I had learned when I was raised was challenged by the new information I was absorbing. I quickly realized that most of what I'd been taught was not the approach I wanted to use.

I embraced what I believe to be a better way of parenting. The results are evident in my children. In many ways, I feel they are more emotionally healthy than I was at their ages. My children have suffered pain and hurts from the divorce that could have wounded them for life. But I believe that by God's grace they are becoming stronger and better adults because of a higher level of understanding of how God works in their lives. This is the godly wisdom that I prayed for, and I have every confidence that God will continue the good work that He has started in us.

Growing in Love

One of the hardest lessons for me was patience. It is difficult to let someone or something take its course without rushing in and taking charge. Standing back and waiting to give yourself time to make a good decision is not easy. I have not perfected this approach, but I am aware of how much better I can handle situations when I use it. Being the mother of five children has certainly given me an abundance of opportunities for practice.

Patience also developed in me a greater tolerance for and acceptance of differences in each of my children. At times, Rachel was a picky eater. It had been ingrained in me while I was growing up that cleaning my plate at dinner was a major issue. If I didn't, I would get in trouble. I actually started out parenting Bethanee and Dana with the same rigid rules. By the time Rachel came along, though, I began to change my parenting approach.

There were times when I tried to force Rachel to eat something. On occasion, I would even let her sit in her high chair for hours, and she would usually fall asleep there. Time made no difference to her. She would not eat something unless she wanted to.

Finally I thought, *Beth, why are you doing this? Why are you making eating such a big, emotional trial for Rachel? If the peanut butter and jelly will fill her up as well as meat and potatoes, then why not give her the peanut butter and jelly?*

It seems simple, but it was absolutely revolutionary to my way of thinking. Being tolerant with Rachel about what she ate seemed to contradict everything I had been brought up to believe. When I was growing up, mealtimes could be miserable for me if I was being asked to eat things I hated, such as green peppers and sweet potatoes. I hate them to this day, and it's a big family joke. But the Lord had been teaching me to let those things go, and by the time Rachel came along, I learned not to be such an absolute authority.

Rachel must have sensed that the desire of my heart was to be faithful to the Lord and raise my children with as much godly influence as possible. The following tribute to me was found a week or so after her death and given to me as Mother's Day approached. Nothing has brought me greater comfort than to have Rachel's thoughts of how she really felt about me, knowing that I will never have her with me again in this life. She left me a priceless gift with these words. I still weep when I see them. Oh, how I loved this little girl!

> • Sacrifice should be her name. Because she has given up so much for us.
> • Humble should be her name. Because she will never admit the great thing she has done.
> • Faith should be her name. Because she has enough to carry us, as well as herself, through this crazy world.
> • Strength should be her name. Because she had enough to bear and take care for five children.
> • Wisdom should be her name. Because her words and knowledge are worth more than gold.
> • Beautiful should be her name. Because it is not only evident in her face, but in her heart and soul as well.
> • Graceful should be her name. Because she carries herself as a true woman of God.

> • Loving should be her name. Because of the deepness of each hug and kiss she gives us.
> • Elizabeth is her name. But I call her giving, humble, faithful, strong, wise, beautiful, graceful, loving mom.

Try a Little Tenderness

These are tough times to be growing up. Life seems to be moving quickly these days, and complex things come at kids from many directions. Parents often don't know what to do, and tragedies like the Columbine killings make some parents even more frantic to find a guaranteed way to produce perfect kids.

In the wake of the killings, many people began turning their attention to the impact of negative music and violent video games. I have always had guidelines for my kids in all of those areas because I want them to have good influences in their lives and not let their values be sabotaged by all the media garbage—violence, sexual overtones, and immorality—that is out there.

I have come to the point of seeing that the rules go only to a certain point, and after that, our children need to have enough of a moral foundation that they can choose what's going to be a good and healthy influence and steer away from things that are going to hurt them.

Unfortunately I feel as a parent, there are times that I experience a lack of understanding or knowledge of where my children really are emotionally. I may not understand the unbearable pressures they are faced with, primarily because their teenage issues are so different from what I faced at that age. I know my inadequacies to deal with certain topics are enhanced when I do not feel well informed on the subject. This creates in me a tendency to view everything from my own narrow perspective rather than take the time to figure out what the healthy and safe course of action is.

One thing is for sure: my children were going to experiment with the boundaries between right and wrong. They were going to be very curious about what was going on outside the walls of their home and the church. Instead of feeling frantic and desperate, causing myself to overreact in those situations, I let go of the rope just a bit. My goal was not to smother or strangle them with my rules and overprotectiveness; rather, I wanted to be there as support with safe guidelines. Believe me, my mother's heart was in anguish trying to practice this.

I want my kids to know that good and evil are real, that there are safe things and dangerous things. But most of all, I want them to know there's a safe place with me in our home and they can come to me and enjoy my covering and my protection.

Some of the best times with Rachel occurred when she came to me and said, "Mom, you're not going to be proud of me for this, but I did something I shouldn't have." I almost cried with joy when she trusted me enough to come to me with her flaws and failures.

That's the way I want my children to be with me, and I think it's the way God wants His children to be with Him. Our parenting should mirror God's love for us, His patience with our failures, and His amazing grace, which restores us to a right relationship with Him.

10 Anatomy of a Tragedy

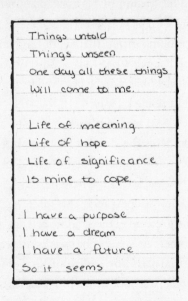

Things untold
Things unseen
One day all these things
Will come to me.

Life of meaning
Life of hope
Life of significance
Is mine to cope.

I have a purpose
I have a dream
I have a future
So it seems

According to the folks who knew him best, seventeen-year-old Dylan Klebold was pretty much like most other high school kids, only nicer.

A friendly kid who was born into a loving, affluent home and who joined the Boy Scouts and played Little League during his younger years, Klebold had attended Columbine's prom three nights before the shooting, telling his friends that he hoped they wouldn't lose touch with each other when they all went off to college that fall.

There were subtle signs that not everything was as placid as it seemed. Klebold, whose mother was Jewish, sometimes surprised his bowling buddies when, after rolling a ball down the lane, he would say, "Heil Hitler!" They thought he was joking.

Klebold and his friend Eric Harris had a run-in with the law after they were caught burglarizing a van. And the teen was part of a Columbine group that wore long coats and called themselves the Trench Coat Mafia. Still, no one who knew him suspected Klebold could be involved in something as horrible as the Columbine killings.

The story of Eric Harris is more complex and confusing. An excellent student who dazzled his English teachers, Harris had a good sense of humor that he would use to entertain coworkers at Blackjack Pizza, where he and Klebold worked.

But Harris knew sadness too. The son of a decorated military veteran, he grew up in the shadow of a successful and athletic older brother. At school, he was routinely taunted and called homosexual names by athletes, who seemed to have free rein at Columbine, a school with a top-notch athletic program.

Harris vented his rage by pulling pranks on neighbors, playing hour after hour of violent video games, listening to nihilistic rock music, and railing against his perceived enemies on the Web site he created.

"I will rig up explosives all over a town and detonate each one of them at will after I mow down a whole f****** area full of you snotty a** rich mother f****** highstrung godlike attitude having worthless piece of s*** whores," he wrote in 1998 in one of many virulent entries on his site, which was shut down by America Online in the days after the tragedy.

"I don't care if I live or die in the shoot-out. All I want to do is kill and injure as many of you p***** as I can."

A year before the Columbine shootings that would make him a national antihero, Harris began translating his fantasies into action, using a notebook to keep detailed notes and diagrams of his planned assault, which would require plenty of guns and bullets, along with nearly one hundred bombs. The conflagration took place, as scheduled, on the anniversary of Adolf Hitler's birthday.

In the days and weeks after Columbine, the event was analyzed and debated by hundreds of journalists, politicians, and self-appointed experts. Over time, the debaters seemed to point to two main culprits: the mass media and guns.

Campaigning for the presidency in the days after the tragedy, independent candidate Pat Buchanan struck out at the entertainment industry, saying, "Hollywood bears a measure of responsibility." Days later, Time Warner Chairman Gerald Levin struck back: "Where's the cry to stop the proliferation of guns?"

But for the parents of one of the victims, the tragedy raises deeper questions about the problems that caused the killings and what we can do about them.

Darrell

Kids in Chaos

People always ask me my opinion about what caused the two killers to go on their rampage that day. In a sense, an event like this defies analysis. However, I think several common denominators emerge.

For one, it seems that Dylan Klebold was powerfully affected by peer pressure. According to published accounts, people who knew him say he was a follower. Peer pressure has been around as long as there have been teenagers, but somehow kids didn't kill each other in schools back in the fifties and sixties. Obviously other things have changed. But I believe that in this case, peer pressure was a factor. Perhaps schools and churches can help address this issue, diffusing it somewhat and encouraging kids to stand on their own two feet instead of being followers.

I also wonder about a second issue—the possibility of improving parental intervention. It seems to me that as a society we spent less time with our children in the '90s than we did in the '50s and '60s.

When considering this issue, I can't help but compare the lives of Cassie Bernall and Eric Harris.

Cassie's mom went into her daughter's room where she found a stack of letters from a friend. Reading the letters, she was shocked to discover that Cassie was involved in witchcraft and had even talked of killing her own parents. Cassie's parents confronted Cassie, restricted her freedom, demanded that she quit seeing some of her old friends who had exerted a negative influence on her, and monitored her behavior very carefully. As it turned out, things went much better than they expected. Cassie's life was transformed, and in the last years of her life, she became a positive, moral teenager.

Compare that to Eric Harris's situation. According to published accounts, for much of the year before the killings, Eric had numerous bombs and large amounts of bomb-making materials, guns, and ammunition in his basement. Eric showed off much of this arsenal on some of the videotapes he and Dylan had made in the months before the killings. How I wish Eric's parents had intervened as Cassie's parents did.

We can't turn back the clock and attempt to re-create the world of *Leave It to Beaver*. The '50s and '60s are gone, and there's nothing we can do about that. And even those supposedly golden years had their problems. But we can spend more time with our children. And I'm not talking about so-called quality time. There is no such thing as quality time without good old quantity time.

A Spiritual Vacuum

In the end, I believe the most crucial factor leading to the Columbine tragedy was that many young people today have been raised in a culture where there is a complete lack of moral or spiritual exposure.

Prior to the '60s, it was fairly common for children to pray in school, to read the Bible at school, or to recite the Pledge of Allegiance, which said Americans were "one nation under God." But during the '60s, a series of controversial Supreme Court decisions changed all that. During this time, "separation of church and state" became a household term.

Now, many of our taxpayer-supported public schools are virtual religion-free zones. As a nation, we have lost something important and intangible that cannot be brought back by the Supreme Court. We are living within a society that has lost any sense of consciousness of right and wrong. We have lost the awareness that our lives and actions are being scrutinized by a Supreme Being beyond ourselves.

In my day, schools taught that Thanksgiving commemorates the time when the Pilgrims gave thanks to God for bringing them to a place where they could practice religious freedom. I asked several young people recently what they had been taught about Thanksgiving in school. They said they were told that Thanksgiving commemorates the time when the Pilgrims thanked the Indians for the turkeys they ate. My response is, "What turkey taught you that?" This is not the complete story of American history. In this and many other ways, we have removed any trace of a spiritual influence from our country and our schools.

If you put these things together—particularly peer pressure and a pervasive lack of consciousness about God, spirituality, and right and wrong—you've got an extremely dangerous combination.

I believe Rachel attempted to describe the craziness of our current situation in her journal.

People are crying,
Losing their minds.
People are dying,
Taking their lives.
Will anyone save them?
Will anyone help?
Will somebody listen,
Or am I all by myself?

Please reach out your hand,
Grab a hold of their life.
Open their eyes,
To His wonderful light.
Let them know,
Of His undying love.
That this comes only,
From Heaven Above.

Please reach out your hand,
Grab a hold of their life.
Don't let go,
Without a good fight.
Witness to them,
Show them the way.
Give them God's love,
And give it today.

I sit here and tell you,
To go save a life.
But what am I doing
To give that good fight?
I judge other souls,
Never checking my own.
Oh my Lord,
I should have known.

In the wake of Columbine, political leaders were willing to examine all kinds of ways of making the schools safer for our kids. Some said schools needed more security guards and X-ray machines. Others said the problem was lack of strong gun control laws, a subject I'll discuss later.

My plea to these leaders is this: We're willing to look at various things as possible solutions, but why aren't we willing to look at the possibility that some of the problems we are facing today result from our vanishing consciousness of a supernatural being?

I have attended a number of legislative sessions around the country in the past year. Many of these sessions open with prayer, but the very same legislators who sit in these sessions won't allow their kids to pray in school. Does that sound like hypocrisy to anybody besides me?

Beth

The Flames of Hate

Like Darrell, I see the role of peer pressure and our seemingly godless culture in this tragedy. But for me it comes back to the killers themselves. Eric Harris and Dylan Klebold were two very misguided, very misdirected, and very lost souls.

People are desperate to try to fix all the blame somewhere, but I think we ought to look at how the two boys had a self-perpetuating hate. Just about everybody gets picked on at school or in life, but those boys fed their hurts and insecurities until they became a powerful hate.

They chose that hate, they thrived on it, and it burned within them like a fire that could not be snuffed out. The fire burned so hot that it made them inaccessible to anybody who tried to offer them any affection or kindness, as I know Rachel did. I'm sure that at times teachers tried to reach out to them too.

Their parents must have tried to reach the boys. And I believe they would have attempted to find a way to help their sons if they had known they were so hate filled. But the boys chose hate over anything else, and that choice totally blocked them from receiving anything that would have softened their hearts to any degree or in any way.

Our society isn't perfect, and perhaps we all bear a share of the blame for what happened at Columbine. There is certainly enough to go around. We feed our kids a steady diet of hatred and violence. That's what they are being raised on. People think it's entertaining, and those boys were entertaining themselves with some pretty nasty material.

The only thing that was different between the violence they watched and enjoyed on TV monitors and the killings they perpetrated on April 20 is that real violence has real consequences. The Columbine shootings killed, injured, and traumatized innocent people. They didn't come with a pause command or a reset button. It wasn't a game that anyone could start over again when things got out of hand. Columbine involved real destruction and real consequences, and at times I wonder whether some kids know the difference.

Darrell

Guns and Gun Control

As I watched one of the killers' videos they laughed about gun control. Eric Harris looked at the camera and said, "You know what's going to happen is, they're going to pass stricter gun laws." He began using a lot of foul language at that point, then he said, "Let the mother f****** do whatever they want to, but that's not the issue. Because guys like us are going to get them no matter what."

The last week of January 2000 was a big week for gun control efforts. In Washington, President Bill Clinton gave his final State of the Union address, and one of his invited guests in the audience was Tom Mauser, whose fifteen-year-old son Daniel was killed at Columbine. With Tom Mauser looking on, the president promised to work for an aggressive new slate of crime and violence measures, including $280 million for new gun enforcement programs.

Meanwhile, back in Colorado, members of the state House of Representatives were debating gun control legislation, one of many bills introduced in the Colorado legislature in the wake of the Columbine killings.

A major development was the stunning testimony of Robyn Anderson, who went to a Denver area gun show in late 1998 to help Dylan Klebold and Eric Harris buy three of the guns they used in the killings. At the time, Anderson was eighteen and the two boys were seventeen.

"It was entirely too easy," said Anderson, who stated that none of the sellers seemed the least bit concerned about the two underage boys who were handling the guns and asking the dealers all the questions. "They bought guns from three sellers," said Anderson. "They were all private. They paid cash. There was no receipt. I was not asked any questions at all. There was no background check. All I had to do was show my driver's license to prove that I was eighteen."

Another Chamber, Another Hearing

Some of the parents who had lost children at Columbine attended the gun control hearing, but I wasn't among them. I was testifying in another chamber, where legislators were debating a bill that called for the posting of the Ten Commandments in Colorado's public schools.

Even though the Ten Commandments legislation failed to pass, the fact that I was at that hearing and not the gun control hearing says a lot about my views on things. I know there are many, many problems in the world, but I'm sure that the problem is not guns. I get angry that people attempt to slap legislative Band-Aids on our country's gaping social and spiritual wounds, and that politicians jump on the antigun bandwagon when a tragedy like Columbine occurs.

In May 1999, about one month after the Columbine killings, I went to Washington where I spoke at a hearing of the Judiciary Committee. Everybody wanted to find a scapegoat for the tragedy, and the National Rifle Association (NRA) was a convenient target because the organization was having its national convention in Denver at the time. I was not there to defend the NRA. I was there to say that these are not the people to blame. Guns are not the reason people die. The reason people die is that there is murder in the hearts of other people.

Here's part of what I told the committee that day:

Descendants of Cain

Since the dawn of creation there have been both good and evil in the hearts of men and women. We all contain the seeds of kindness or the seeds of violence.

The death of my wonderful daughter, Rachel Joy Scott, and the deaths of that heroic teacher and the other eleven children must not be in vain. Their blood cries out for answers.

The first recorded act of violence in human history was when Cain slew his brother Abel out in a field. The villain was not the club he used. Neither was it the NCA, the National Club Association. The true killer was Cain, and the reason for the murder could only be found in Cain's heart.

I am not a member of the NRA. I am not a hunter. I do not even own a gun. I am not here to represent or defend the NRA, but I don't believe that they are responsible for my daughter's death. If I believed they had anything to do with Rachel's murder I would be their strongest opponent.

I am here today to declare that Columbine was not just a tragedy—it was a spiritual event that should force us to look at where the real blame lies.

Much of the blame lies here in this room. Much of that blame lies behind the pointing fingers of the accusers themselves. I wrote a poem four nights ago, before I knew I would be speaking here today, that expresses my feelings best:

> Your laws ignore our deepest needs
> Your words are empty air
> You've stripped away our heritage
> You've outlawed simple prayer
> Now gunshots fill our classrooms
> And precious children die

> You seek for answers everywhere
> And ask the question "Why?"
> You regulate restrictive laws
> Through legislative creed
> And yet you fail to understand
> That God is what we need!

Spiritual influences were present within our educational system for most of our nation's history. Many of our major colleges began as theological seminaries. This is a historic fact.

What has happened to us as a nation? We have refused to honor God, and in doing so, we have opened the doors to hatred and violence . . .

I challenge every young person in America and around the world to realize that on April 20th, 1999, at Columbine High School, prayer was brought back to our schools. Do not let the many prayers offered by those students be in vain . . .

My daughter's death will not be in vain. The young people of this country will not allow that to happen.

Eric and Dylan planned their rampage for a year. Their weapon of choice was not guns, but bombs using propane gas tanks. This is something we keep forgetting. Most of their bombs did not work, but if they had been successful, would we have heard outrage about people using gas containers? Would we outlaw barbecue grills? Would politicians jump on the bandwagon with that? Of course not. People already had an agenda about guns. Columbine only gave them more publicity.

Beth

Laws Can't Change Hearts

During the year that they planned their killing spree and during the morning they unleashed their violence, Eric Harris and Dylan Klebold violated eighteen laws before the April 20 incident ever happened. Realistically speaking, I think we probably already have every gun law that we need to prevent the misuse of guns.

The problem is far deeper, something that is in people's hearts. We are trying to legislate the morals and the actions of our society through more gun control laws. That approach is doomed to fail.

Guns are too easily accessible. I have no doubt about that. I wish with all my heart that they were less accessible, but people always find ways to get around the law. Tightening our gun control laws may deter a few criminals, but people who really are bent on committing acts of violence with weapons will find a way to get what they need in order to accomplish their purposes.

It's just too bad that we're so desensitized and we're so hardened in our consciences that guns are used for personal violence, personal vengeance, and personal crime.

To me, the real issues here are the issues of the heart, and no amount of legislation can affect the heart. Only God can do that. But as good citizens, we can modify and change things that have proved to be detrimental to our society.

In July 1999, I wrote a letter about these issues to Rev. Rob Schenck, who is with a group called the Ten Commandments. The group works to make our nation aware of our

Judeo-Christian moral heritage once again. Here is what I said in that letter:

In June of 1962 legislation was enacted which stripped our public schools of prayer. The prayer which was banned by this
unwise decision was simply: "Almighty God, we acknowledge
our dependence upon Thee, and beg Thy blessing upon us, our
parents, our teachers, and our country." This action sabotaged
the safety and future well-being of generations to come. We
have now inherited the bitter fruit. Teen violence, crime, and
pregnancies rose dramatically, while academic scores have
plummeted. The Duke of Wellington once said, "If you divorce
religion from education, you produce a race of clever devils."
Nowhere have we seen this more clearly demonstrated than
here in Littleton, Colorado.

For years now, our children have been fed a constant diet of
violence through television, movies, and video games. They
have been exposed to an entirely new set of values, which glo-
rify hedonism, sexual promiscuity, and violence as a means of
conflict management. Some of our youth have learned these
new values well, and are now acting out their frustrations and
anger in the most horrible acts of murder and violence.

Where do we go from here? We must recapture our nation's
great spiritual inheritance of Judeo-Christian values. We must
have a change of heart, which of necessity must begin with the
nurture of the family unit. Support and encouragement must
be given to fathers and mothers to raise their children with
godly values and respect for human life, beginning at concep-
tion. New legislation and more laws cannot guarantee a

changed society, only a true change of heart will ensure that. Government should merely encourage and empower what we the people, as a nation conceived under God, must be responsible to uphold. Most important, the laws of our land should never be in contradiction to the laws of God.

The down payment for the change we so desperately need in our nation has been paid by the blood of my daughter, Rachel, and the other precious children killed or wounded at Columbine. The grim spiritual darkness, which now covers our nation, has been challenged by the light of our children, several of whom willingly laid down their lives for the cause of Jesus Christ. Our nation must come to grips with the fact that almighty God, our Creator, will call us into account for the elimination of His word and counsel. It's time for those God-honoring leaders of our nation to once again rise to the challenge before us and let their voice be heard. May that voice rise to a chorus, refusing to be turned away or once again intimidated into silence!

The courage to stand for godly truth, in a time and place where you may feel you are standing alone, can best be drawn from my daughter Rachel's own words, penned in her personal journal only a few days before her untimely young death on April 20, 1999.

> I'm drowning
> In my own lake of despair.
> I'm choking
> My hands wrapped around my neck.
> I'm dying

> Quickly my soul leaves, slowly my body withers.
> It isn't suicide,
> I consider it homicide.
> The world you have created has lead to my death.

Written by Rachel Joy Scott in April of 1999

As a mother of a slain child, slaughtered in the tragedy at Columbine High School, I plead for public repentance from our nation's leaders for removing God's influence from our schools. Please, I beg you, do not let my daughter's sacrifice be in vain. I conclude with these immortal words drawn from President Abraham Lincoln's speech at Gettysburg, Pennsylvania, on November 19, 1863, who stated so eloquently: "It is rather for us to be here dedicated to the great task remaining before us . . . that from these honored dead we take increased devotion to that cause for which they gave the last full measure of devotion . . . that we here highly resolved that these dead shall not have died in vain."

Later, Larry and I were able to discuss some of our concerns with President Clinton who, along with other national leaders, has talked about the tragedy of Columbine.

But reclaiming our nation's moral heritage isn't something we should leave up to national leaders because it isn't a political challenge. It's a spiritual challenge. It's a moral challenge.

Reclaiming our heritage is a job that all of us should do. I ask you to join me right now in the crusade to bring a renewed sense of godliness back to our homes, our schools, and our nation.

God,
    Where are you? What should I do?
Jesus, I call upon your name?
Deliver me from my ways.

RACHEL

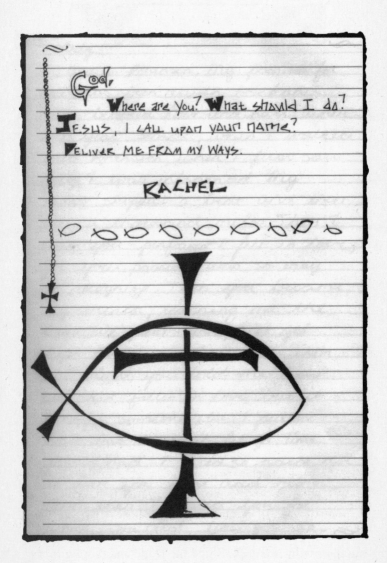

11 Your Life, Your Choice

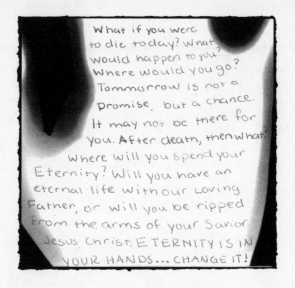

What if you were to die today? What would happen to you? Where would you go? Tommorrow is not a promise, but a chance. It may not be there for you. After death, then what? Where will you spend your Eternity? Will you have an eternal life with our Loving Father, or will you be ripped from the arms of your Savior Jesus Christ. ETERNITY IS IN YOUR HANDS... CHANGE IT!

During the 1990s, schools in American towns such as West Paducah, Kentucky; Pearl, Mississippi; Jonesboro, Arkansas; and Springfield, Oregon, became infamous as places where some students had lost their lives and many others had lost their innocence and their hope.

Columbine, which endured its tragedy near the end of the decade, has earned the unwanted distinction of being the site of the nation's most deadly school shooting.

It is senseless to compare one tragedy to another. To anyone who has lost a child or loved one in such horrible circumstances, no comparison is possible. The grief is incalculable.

Nevertheless, the destruction and severity of the Columbine attack struck deep in the hearts of many people, causing psychic tremors around the world and causing many to look deep into their hearts and cry out, "What in God's name has happened, and why?"

One writer eloquently stated in the pages of *Time* magazine, "With each passing day of shock and grief you could almost hear the church bells tolling in the background, calling the country to a different debate, a careful conversation in which even Presidents and anchormen behave as though they are in the presence of something bigger than they are."

In the year since April 20, 1999, both Darrell Scott and Beth Nimmo have traveled around the country talking to thousands of young people and adults who want to hear their story.

DARRELL
SPEAKING

In their many talks and media events, Rachel's parents have challenged their listeners to confront perhaps the ultimate issue facing the human race: the ongoing battle between the forces of good and evil. The Columbine tragedy has helped to expose the differences between good and evil with a brilliant light.

Darrell

Two People, Two Paths

When I talk to groups around the country, I ask them to consider how a young man named Eric Harris and a young woman named Rachel Scott followed two diverging paths in their lives.

Those paths, which went in such opposite directions, crossed with fatal finality on April 20, 1999. Four bullets from Eric Harris's gun killed Rachel.

These two young people were born just days apart. They lived just a few miles away from each other. But in many ways, they couldn't have been more different.

Eric Harris was a bitter, angry person who went out of his way to give voice to his inward bitterness. His Web site and his prerampage videos are seething monuments to one boy's hate. Much of the time, he seemed to hate nearly everything he saw in this world, including himself.

YOUNG PEOPLE RESPONDING TO DARRELL'S MESSAGE

Looking at Rachel's writings takes one to the completely opposite end of the spectrum. Repeatedly in her journals, she chose love; she chose compassion; she chose to serve God with a passion. Some people are uncomfortable using terms like *good* and *evil*, but how else should we describe the opposing inner motivations and outward behaviors of these two young people?

I believe that spiritual forces were at work to take Eric to the level of hatred and despair that he experienced. Eric may not have known this at the time, but Satan doesn't always reveal his hand. That's why he is called the great deceiver.

Spiritual forces of another sort were at work to prepare my daughter for what happened to her. I believe with all of my heart that God had His hand on Rachel from the moment she was born until the moment she died.

And both Eric and Rachel used the same phrase to describe what they were trying to do with their lives. Both talked about starting a "chain reaction."

For an assignment in one of her classes at Columbine, Rachel wrote a paper entitled "My Ethics, My Codes of Life." The paper is a virtual catalog of the core values Rachel held most dear: trust, honesty, compassion, love, and the desire to believe the best about people. She concluded her paper by saying: "My codes may seem like a fantasy that can never be reached, but test them for yourself, and see the kind of effect they have in the lives of people around you. You just may start a chain reaction."

In one video that Eric recorded with Dylan Klebold in the months before their rampage, Eric spoke of a quite different type of chain reaction. Through his actions on April 20, Eric hoped to kill hundreds of innocent students and thereby unleash a period of chaos and terror.

A Chain of Choices

Eric Harris probably didn't start out life deciding he wanted to be a mass murderer. Rather, his life took shape step-by-step as he made decisions all along the way.

Neither did Rachel announce on her first birthday that she wanted to be a devoted disciple of Jesus. Instead, it was through a series of fits and starts that she decided, over a period of years, to gradually give more and more of herself to God.

In one of her earlier journal entries, Rachel weighed the choices she faced as a young person in contemporary America. She could give in to easy pleasure, or she could submit her life to Christ. She chose the latter, as you can see.

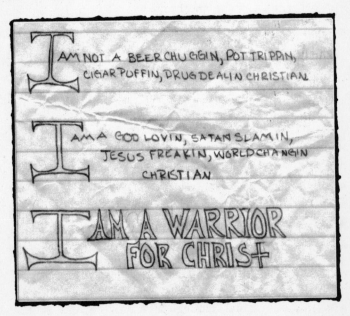

I AM NOT A BEER CHUGGIN, POT TRIPPIN, CIGAR PUFFIN, DRUG DEALIN CHRISTIAN

I AM A GOD LOVIN, SATAN SLAMIN, JESUS FREAKIN, WORLD CHANGIN CHRISTIAN

I AM A WARRIOR FOR CHRIST

Rachel also encouraged others to make the best choices when they faced important decisions in their lives. She repeatedly encouraged her friends to consider the decisions of the present moment in the light of eternity.

A year before her death, Rachel wrote a letter to a friend named Brittney. In that letter, Rachel said, "Eternity is not just looking to the future and our place with God in Heaven, but it is looking at our Eternity as if it were only moments away." A few lines later, Rachel added, "People are not aware that tomorrow is not a promise, but a chance."

Near the end of the letter, Rachel challenged Brittney to be on the lookout for opportunities to share her faith, opportunities that Rachel believed would make themselves available very soon: "I just feel that there are going to be so many chances for you to witness to people, and they are coming up soon. Be ready for them, they are not far. Be ready."

Today, both Rachel's words and the example of her life challenge us to choose the good path and to tell others about it whenever we can. Will you join me in accepting Rachel's challenge?

Beth

Choosing to Forgive

In the year since Rachel's death, I have found it difficult to follow Christ's command to forgive the killers. Forgiveness has been a daily battle for me. Sometimes it has even been a moment-by-moment struggle. From the beginning I have asked the Lord to give me real forgiveness for Eric and Dylan, but that desire is repeatedly tested.

When *Time* magazine did a cover story about the killers' videotapes and published it at Christmastime, I cried for weeks. I felt so much anger and personal hurt knowing what they said. Later, when Larry and Darrell found out that Rachel was on their target list, I struggled with being very unforgiving and very bitter.

The more knowledge I had about the two boys, the more violated I felt, and the more grace it took for me to walk in forgiveness.

One year after Rachel's death, forgiveness for me is not a one-time act of my will, but it's a choice I make on an ongoing basis. I choose constantly to forgive, even when I don't want to. I choose constantly to lay down my pain because I trust that God is going to do something incredibly beautiful through all this.

Darrell

Rachel's Tears

I woke up at 4:30 one morning about a month after Rachel's funeral. I felt as though God were physically in the room with me, and two scriptures from the Bible were ringing in my mind. It was as though He were speaking them to me. They were, "I have brought you to the kingdom for such a time as this," and "I will put you before kings and leaders and you will not be afraid of what to say. I will put words in your mouth." I know how presumptuous this may sound, but it is the truth.

I began to feel a sense of purpose and destiny over the next few days that wouldn't go away. I had been raised in a pentecostal home and had later moved away from my denominational roots to simply be known as a believer in Jesus rather than be labeled and categorized in any one group. I have wonderful fellowship with a cross-culture of Christians from Seventh-Day Adventists to Baptists to pentecostals and charismatics to Catholics. I do have personal convictions and beliefs, but I do not allow them to dictate the people that God brings across my path. The church that I personally attend is nondenominational, and the pastor has been a dear friend and supporter.

I had stepped away from full-time ministry as a teacher when it became apparent that my marriage was headed for the divorce court. I had closed the door on that part of my life and never again did I expect to publicly speak and minister to groups of people. So when I began to feel a call to move back into a ministry format, it scared me. I had a great job, loved the people I worked with, and had established a good residual income that would eventually allow me to retire and play golf without worrying about finances.

Several days after this experience of sensing God speaking to me, I sat on the edge of my bed one morning and prayed out loud. I said, "God, I want to do whatever You are calling me to do, but I have two requests. I do not want to open my own doors to speaking engagements, and I don't want to wear suits. I prefer comfortable clothes such as jeans."

Within minutes of that prayer, the phone rang. It was a man by the name of Frank Amedia, who had seen Rachel's funeral on CNN a month earlier. What he said over the next few minutes altered my life forever. First of all, he said that he had been praying for me faithfully since Rachel's funeral. He said that the Lord had shown him that I was going to be raised up to speak to leaders and young people all across this country. As a prosperous businessman, he wanted to lend his financial support to whatever God was calling me to do. That was the first of many confirmations I received about my future.

However, what he said next was to become a major contribution to Rachel's testimony from beyond the grave. He said that three times in his life, he had had dreams that he knew were from God. The first two had to do with his business, which had spread across the United States rapidly. His third dream took place shortly after Rachel's funeral. He dreamed about her eyes and a flow of tears that were watering something that he couldn't quite see in the dream. He was adamant about the eyes and tears and wanted to know if that meant anything to me. He was disappointed when I said, "No, Frank, I don't have any idea what that means." He told me that the dream had haunted him for days, and he knew there was a reason for it. He asked if I would take his phone number and call him if I could ever shed light on what he felt was a real vision from God. I consented, and we hung up.

Several days passed, and I forgot about my conversation with Frank. Then I got a call from the sheriff's department letting me know that they were ready to release Rachel's backpack that she had on when she was murdered. There was a bullet hole through her backpack, and they had held it for evidence to determine whose gun the bullet had come from.

We suspected that Rachel's final diary was still in the backpack, but there were two of them. One of them had a bullet hole entering at a place on the back cover where she had written the words "I WON'T BE LABELED AS AVERAGE." I wept uncontrollably as I read what she had written on the front cover: "I write, not for the sake of glory, not for the sake of fame, not for the sake of success, but for the sake of my soul—Rachel Joy." Could she have ever suspected that within the next twelve to thirteen months her written words would be heard around the world? That they would be quoted by newscasters across our nation? That they would be printed in book form for the reading of generations of young people yet to be born? But my biggest shock was yet to come!

I turned to the end of her last diary and could not believe what was staring up at me from that final page! A drawing of her eyes with a stream of tears that were watering a rose! Later someone pointed out that there were thirteen clear tears falling from her eyes before they touched the rose and turned into what look like blood drops. There were, of course, thirteen victims of the two murderers. I was so stunned that I could barely breathe. A week ago, a complete stranger who lived more than one thousand miles away had described exactly what I was looking at in Rachel's final diary! I sat for thirty-five to forty-five minutes in my truck and prayed for God to help me understand what was happening.

My prayers were answered—but not immediately. We discovered that same rose in a previous diary drawn a year before Rachel's death. The first drawing simply showed the rose with the bloodlike drops, not her eyes or the clear tears. The first drawing also showed the rose growing up out of a columbine plant. Columbine High School got its name from the state flower. In addition to that, she had drawn a cross with the words: "Greater love hath no man than this, that a man would lay down his life for his friends"!

We had two drawings from a year apart that form a total picture! A scripture verse stating that the greatest love is when one lays down his life for a friend. Beside that verse is a columbine flower, out of which is growing a rose that is being watered by drops of blood that have as their source thirteen clear teardrops from the eyes of a young girl named Rachel.

I believe with all of my heart that the Columbine tragedy was a spiritual wake-up call to the youth of this generation. We have stripped them of their true heritage by removing all spiritual influences from their schools and passing legislation that violates our country's Constitution, history, and moral foundations.

Two thousand years ago a Teacher (Jesus Christ) and twelve students (disciples) brought permanent change to Planet Earth. At the end of this past millennium, another teacher and twelve students gripped the attention of the human race. That first Teacher was called "the Son of David." That last teacher's name was David. That first Teacher was called "the Lamb of God." One of those last student's names means "little female lamb." *Rachel* not only means "lamb," but she chose to perform a mime at her high school talent show that was called "Watch the Lamb." That mime would be performed on CNN to the whole world from behind her casket by the young girl who taught it to Rachel.

There are many untold spiritual stories about the Columbine tragedy, but the one that has the most impact on the youth that I speak to is the story of the rose. I shared that story in Jackson, Tennessee, several weeks after I first saw Rachel's drawing. At the end of the meeting a young girl came up to me just sobbing. She said, "Mr. Scott, I did not know what you were going to talk about before you came, but I had felt impressed to have you read some verses from the Bible, and here they are." She handed me her Bible, and it was opened to Jeremiah 31:15–17 (NASB):

> Thus says the LORD,
> "A voice is heard in Ramah,

Lamentation and bitter weeping.
Rachel is weeping for her children;
She refuses to be comforted for her children,
Because they are no more."
Thus says the LORD,
"Restrain your voice from weeping,
And your eyes from tears;
For your work shall be rewarded," declares the LORD,
"And they shall return from the land of the enemy.
And there is hope for your future," declares the LORD,
"And your children shall return to their own territory."

When I read these words, the door of closure slammed shut in my spirit. I knew from that moment that Rachel's death was not in vain. I knew that this teacher and twelve students were going to have an eternal impact on the lives of many people. I knew that the columbine flower Rachel had drawn represented the tragedy out of which the youth of this generation (the rose) would emerge, anointed by the very tears of God Himself that were pictured flowing from Rachel's eyes. This tragedy shall be turned into triumph by the grace of God!

Appendix
Picking Up the Torch

At Rachel's funeral, Pastor Bruce Porter issued a powerful challenge to all who heard him:

Young people here today, hear me. I want to issue a challenge to each and every one of you. Don't despair of life; don't despair of what has happened to you.

Rachel carried a torch, the torch of truth, the torch of compassion, the torch of love, the torch of the good news of Jesus Christ, her Savior and Lord, who she was not ashamed of even in her hour of death.

I want to lay a challenge before each and every one of you

young people here today. The torch has fallen from Rachel's hand. Who will pick it up again? Who will pick up the torch again?

In the following year, several efforts sprang up to honor the memory of Rachel and the other Columbine victims and to carry on their work.

The Columbine Redemption was founded to proclaim the truth that Columbine was a spiritual event. The organization publishes a monthly magazine called *Rachel's Journal,* which profiles Columbine victims and reports on some of the activities of youth and memorial activities around the country.

For information, visit the organization's Web site (www.thecolumbineredemption.com), or write:

> The Columbine Redemption
> 137 W. Country Line Road
> Littleton, CO 80129

This organization is also raising funds for a permanent Columbine Memorial/Training Center to be created near the school. To contribute, write or call (303) 346-1300.

For information about Rachel Joy Scott, please visit her Web site (www.rachelscott.com or rachelschallenge.com).

Both Darrell and Beth are also involved with Pastor Bruce Porter's Torchgrab Youth Ministries. We wish to thank him for his support.

Speaking engagements for Darrell Scott and Beth Nimmo are handled exclusively by Ambassador Speakers Bureau, Nashville, TN; 615-370-4700.